Classroom STRATEGIES *for* Interactive Learning

DOUG BUEHL

AUTHOR

A Monograph of the Wisconsin State Reading Association

1995 • Fourth Printing

Acknowledgements

A number of individuals deserve recognition for their roles in this publication. Bill Hurley, editor of the *WEAC News & Views*, developed the concept of a regular column in that newspaper that would appeal to classroom teachers looking for ideas useful to their teaching. His support has allowed these strategy columns to be shared with teachers throughout the state. My colleague at Madison East High School, Sharon McPike, thoughtfully read and critiqued each strategy before it went to press. I continue to value her input in "reality testing" what I write. Dr. Richard Telfer, Professor of Education at the University of Wisconsin–Whitewater, reviewed the manuscript and offered a number of suggestions for clarification and improvement. My wife, Wendy Buehl, also reviewed this manuscript, with a keen eye trained for detecting convoluted prose and unclear description.

Doug Vance, reading specialist at Madison La Follette High School, reacted to portions of this manuscript and contributed his usual insightful feedback. My collaborations with Doug over the years on numerous professional projects have laid the ground-work and provided the inspiration for this project. Chris Kingslow, of Port to Print, our electronic publishing firm in Madison, once again provided his high degree of creative professionalism for this project. Finally, students I have worked with over the years at Madison East High School deserve special mention for helping me learn how I could better teach them. They have taught me much more, I suspect, than I have taught them.

— **Doug Buehl**
Madison East High School
Madison, Wisconsin

Contents

Introduction

Picture the following scene in your classroom. One of your students is leaning over an open textbook, her eyes scanning the pages, and at times she is writing in her notebook. From all appearances, she seems to be completing the assignment. But if she is like many of our students today, this will not be a smooth process for her. She may be having difficulty focusing on what is important in the reading. She may be only superficially skimming the textbook, looking for answers needed to satisfy an assignment. She may be frustrated with the amount of information she is encountering and feel that she will never "learn all of this." She may have decided that none of this material has "anything to do with her," so she'll merely get the work done, only to forget most of it once this unit is over.

Teachers are well aware that many of their students do not successfully learn their course content. Conversations around the copy machine and in the teachers lounge frequently focus on dissatisfactions with student performance. Because many of our students founder with classroom reading demands, we may at times lose confidence in reading assignments. We may resort to telling students what they need to know instead of having them read it or we may frequently turn to other media for instruction. Yet significant portions of our curricula are necessarily print-based, and teachers know that our students need to develop effective reading behaviors in order to survive and be successful.

During the last decade, Wisconsin has witnessed a number of initiatives to help teachers improve student learning in their content fields. The Department of Public Instruction's Curriculum Guide, *Strategic Learning in the Content Areas* (1989), has spawned numerous workshops, in-services, and programs which have explored effective instructional ideas. Likewise, CRISS projects (*Content Reading Including Study Skills*, a National Diffusion Network program) have been implemented in schools throughout the state. Teachers are finding that classroom strategies which directly help students in their reading and learning are making a noticeable difference with many of their students.

This book highlights thirty popular classroom teaching strategies that can be adapted for students from elementary school through high school and which are appropriate for helping students learn in all content areas—from language arts to mathematics, science to foreign language, vocational subjects to social studies. The appeal of these teaching strategies is grounded in their effectiveness in developing students who are active, purposeful, and increasingly independent learners. These strategies also provide innovative ideas for teachers working with diverse classrooms and with students who exhibit a variety of learning needs.

This book is an outgrowth of a four-year collaboration between the Wisconsin State Reading Association and the Wisconsin Education Association Council. During this time, WEAC has sponsored my "Reading Room" column in its monthly newspaper, *News and Views*, which circulates to state public school teachers. The purpose of the column is to provide Wisconsin teachers with information about teaching strategies and practices that they will find useful when working with their students. Teaching strategies featured in the "Reading Room" columns have been selected from a variety of sources, including professional journals, books, and presentations. The columns were written with classroom teachers as an intended audience, with the goal that teachers would be given sufficient information for trying out these strategies with their students without becoming immersed in a lot of "educational jargon." This book represents a collection of these columns.

REFERENCES

Cook, D. (Ed.). (1989). *Strategic learning in the content areas.* Madison, WI: Wisconsin Department of Public Instruction.

Santa, C. (1988). *Content reading including study systems: Reading, writing and studying across the curriculum.* Dubuque, IA: Kendall/Hunt Publishing Company.

Developing Strategic Readers and Learners

CHAPTER 1

An Interactive View of Reading and Learning

Reading comprehension—the process of obtaining meaning from print—is fundamental to learning in the subjects we teach. As teachers we oversee students engaged in some of the behaviors of reading almost daily. And while some of our students appear to handle school reading demands successfully, we realize that many students experience breakdowns in their attempts to make sense of the print they encounter in our classrooms. How can we explain the dynamics involved with being an effective reader? What needs to be happening in a student's mind if reading comprehension is to result? And how can we use teaching strategies to develop readers who can learn from a wide variety of print materials?

Reading Is a Constructive Process. In the past, we described reading comprehension more as a skill than as an active mental process. We conceived reading to be the skill of recognizing letters and words, which led to the ability to connect words into sentences, sentences into paragraphs, and paragraphs into longer discourse which represented various themes or ideas. We regarded getting the main idea, identifying the important details, making inferences, and other such behaviors as being the gist of comprehension. If a student could tell you what was in the text, or in other words **reproduce** what an author had written, then we concluded that comprehension had occurred. If he couldn't, then we turned to explanations such as the student is lacking in reading ability, the student has poor study skills, or the textbook is too difficult.

Recent research in the psychology of reading has led to the development of a much different description of what it means to comprehend a written text. The key concept of this new definition of comprehension is that a reader **constructs** a meaning from a text rather than merely reproduces what is seen on the page. Meaning is something that is actively created rather than passively received. No two people will have exactly the same comprehension of a text because no two people will be reading the text under exactly the same conditions. The four conditions which determine what meaning a reader will construct from a text are:

1. what the **reader** brings to the reading situation;

2. the characteristics of the written **text**;

3. the learning **context** that defines the task and purpose of the reader;

4. the **strategies** consciously applied by the reader to obtain meaning.

Figure 1.1 portrays these four conditions as "The Wisconsin Model of Reading Comprehension" (Cook, 1986, 1989).

FIGURE 1.1

The Wisconsin Model of Reading Comprehension

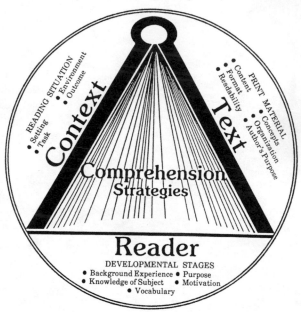

—Cook, D. (Ed.) *Strategic learning in the content areas.* Wisconsin Department of Public Instruction, 1989.

The Reader. The constructive definition of reading emphasizes that it is very simplistic to look at readers solely from the perspective of whether they have developed certain specific reading skills. Reading skills (such as applying phonics, using context, identifying main idea, and so on) are certainly important. But equally important are other traits of the reader. Because comprehension is essentially a mental construction of what is on the page based on what is already known, then the **background knowledge** of the reader is a primary determinant of how a text will be understood. The more a student knows about a topic, the better she will be able to comprehend printed material on that topic. If her background knowledge includes much of the content vocabulary that appears, let's say, in a passage on medieval cathedrals or in an article on creatures that live in the ocean depths, then comprehension is correspondingly enhanced. Comprehension is also greatly influenced by personality characteristics, such a student's personal reasons for reading a piece of print and her willingness or motivation to do so.

The Text. Traditionally, we have talked about the material we ask students to read by referring to readability scores and appropriate reading levels. But readability formulas and grade level designations are not very helpful in predicting how individual students will react to reading a specific piece of prose. Other factors about print which have an impact on reading comprehension need to be considered. The way the content is presented, the density of the concepts, and the study aids which help students focus on important ideas are all crucial. In addition, the language in which the text is written and the text's organizational structure, from the sentence level up through entire chapters or units, play a critical role in the process of constructing meaning. (See Chapter 2 for a discussion of the impact of organizational "text frames" on reading.) Clearly, some texts are written and organized in ways that are much more **considerate** to the reader than others, as anyone who has struggled through a computer manual can attest!

The Context. A reader's comprehension is also influenced by the situation in which the reading occurs. Contextual factors could include physical conditions like whether a room is quiet or noisy, time elements like whether it is early or late in the day, and family circumstances, like whether a child is supported at home in learning. In school, the teacher has a great deal of influence in creating the environment for reading. The teacher's general classroom expectations as well as the instructions for a specific reading determine the way a student approaches a reading task. Does the assignment require a careful examination for mastery of details or will a general understanding of the major ideas be sufficient? Will the information be discussed the next day, tested a week later, or used to complete a project? After the reading, will the

students complete a worksheet, answer inferential questions, write an essay, or conduct a lab experiment? Are students expected to get all that they need on their own, or can they collaborate in their reading with other students? Student comprehension of a text will vary considerably depending on the messages the teacher sends through the context of the reading assignment.

Strategic Reading. Thus comprehension can be seen as a result of a sophisticated interaction among the reader, a specific text, and a context for reading. Effective readers employ **strategies** in order to maneuver meaningfully through this interaction. The strategies a reader selects depend on why she thinks she is reading the selection, how familiar she is with the content of the selection, and of course, what

---

Turning students from passive receivers to active constructors of meaning involves asking them to *use* reading rather than "do" reading.

---

strategies she is skilled in applying. Previewing a selection, rereading a difficult passage, underlining pertinent information, using context to figure out new vocabulary, creating a graphic organizer of a chapter, quizzing oneself, skimming, and taking notes are all examples of effective reading strategies. The more a reader understands **when** certain strategies are effective and **why** they work, the more likely she will become a strategic reader in your classroom.

The following three principles summarize reading as an interactive process among the reader, text, and context. Classroom strategies which embody these three principles are more likely to develop students who can effectively learn from print materials.

1. Students learn best when they have adequate **background knowledge** about a topic. The more the teacher can do to help students understand concepts **prior** to reading about them, the better the students will read. Classroom strategies which shift more of the instruction to the "front" of reading can accomplish a number of important objectives. They can provide the teacher with information about what the students already know and don't know about the topic. They can activate relevant knowledge that will be useful in understanding. They can also build up background with students who are entering a reading with insuffi-

cient knowledge, and they can spotlight key vocabulary. Finally, they can pique student interest in reading about a topic.

2. Students learn best when they are **actively involved** in the reading process. Turning students from passive receivers to active constructors of meaning involves asking them to *use* reading rather than "do" reading. Teaching strategies that encourage students to actively think about what they are reading and to apply what they have learned lead to students more deeply engaged in making sense from print. Activities which permit students to interact with other students tend to increase both motivation to learn and as a result, active involvement.

3. Students learn best when they become **strategic readers**. Teachers ultimately want students to grow from dependence to independence in learning. Students need to discover which learning strategies work best for them and when to apply them. Classroom strategies that guide students in assessing the learning situation, setting their own purpose, choosing the most effective actions, and evaluating their success lead to more self-sufficient individuals capable of becoming lifelong learners.

Frontloading. The importance of **frontloading**—the teaching which is done *before* students are sent into a reading assignment—is underscored in many of the teaching strategies outlined in this book. Frontloading helps prepare students to successfully learn from a reading. Perhaps an analogy will help emphasize the importance of frontloading.

Imagine a student's background knowledge as one of those gray file cabinets standing in the corner of your classroom. The file cabinet represents his memory bank; it contains everything this student knows about the world—his experiences, his perceptions, and his definitions of reality. The contents of the cabinet provide the basis for this student's understanding of what is happening around him. The knowledge in the cabinet is subdivided into drawers, then into sections within the drawers, and finally into file folders within the sections. New information is integrated into these existing mental file folders. If a folder is already bulging with knowledge about a particular topic, reading about that topic will mean adding some new bits of information into an already well-understood folder. However, if the folder for a

particular topic is nearly empty, or if no folder even exists, then the resulting comprehension of a reading will be imprecise, incomplete, and very possibly confused.

By practicing frontloading techniques like building background knowledge, preteaching key vocabulary, focusing attention, setting a reading purpose, and cueing students as to possible effective reading strategies, we are helping students pull the proper file folders from their memories and aiding them in integrating new information into those folders. We are fostering strategic reading behaviors which will lead to successful construction of the meaning of our texts.

Using Effective Teaching Strategies. Teachers are an incredibly resourceful group of people, always on the lookout, it seems, for good ideas and potential materials they can use with their students. Yet, teachers are frequently frustrated with the classroom strategies they see modeled at workshops and conferences, or discussed in professional journals. Although the strategies always seem to work perfectly when they are demonstrated by the "expert," teachers may find it difficult to make them work with their students in real-life classroom situations.

Three rules will help teachers avoid becoming discouraged with using new strategies with their students. *First, what* the students are learning is more important than which strategy is used. Once you have decided what you want students to learn, you can consider how you want to set up instruction. Strategies work well with some objectives and materials, and very poorly with others. Make sure the teaching strategy you chose is aligned with your learning goals.

Second, it's the *thinking* that the students do, not the specific teaching strategy, that counts. Merely following the steps of a strategy does not necessarily guarantee that the students will be engaged in the kind of thinking that will lead to meaningful learning. It's easy for students to fall into a routine of just "going through the motions;" be alert for indications that students are just "doing" rather than thinking. The teaching strategies in this book are not "magic bullets" that inevitably lead to success.

Third, tailor what you are doing to match your students and your goals. Even though classroom strategies are often described in a series of "all-important" steps, be aware of the thinking you want to stimulate in your students, and respond accordingly. Avoid becoming so wrapped up in following a "formula" that you lose sight of the learning that you want to go on in your classroom. Be flexible and adjust how you use any strategy to fit your needs.

FIGURE 1.2

Classroom Teaching Strategies Indexed by **Student Activities**

DEVELOPING VOCABULARY

- Analogy Graphic Organizer
- Concept Definition Mapping
- Frayer Model
- Magnet Summaries
- Possible Sentences
- Semantic Feature Analysis
- Vocabulary Overview Guide

BRAINSTORMING OF IDEAS

- Analogy Graphic Organizer
- Anticipation Guides
- Character Quotes
- Frayer Model
- History Change Frame
- KWL-Plus—Know/Want to Learn/Learned
- LINK—List/Inquire/Note/Know
- Possible Sentences
- PReP—Prereading Plan
- Problematic Situations
- Vocabulary Overview Guide

LEARNING COOPERATIVELY

- Anticipation Guides
- Character Quotes
- Different Perspectives
- Discussion Web
- Follow the Characters
- Point of View Guides
- Problematic Situations
- Save The Last Word For Me
- SMART—Self-Monitoring Approach
  to Reading and Thinking
- Whole Brain Memory Straegies

INTERACTIVE READING

- Anticipation Guides
- Character Quotes
- Different Perspectives
- Discussion Web
- Guided Imagery
- History Change Frame
- Point of View Guides
- Problematic Situations
- Proposition/Support Outlines
- Pyramid Diagram
- Save The Last Word For Me
- Science Connection Overview
- SMART—Self-Monitoring Approach
  to Reading and Thinking
- Story Mapping
- Structured Notetaking

PROMOTING DISCUSSION

- Analogy Graphic Organizer
- Anticipation Guides
- Character Quotes
- Different Perspectives
- Discussion Web
- Follow the Characters
- KWL-Plus—Know/Want to Learn/Learned
- LINK—List/Inquire/Note/Know
- PReP—Prereading Plan
- Problematic Situations
- Pyramid Diagram
- Save The Last Word For Me
- Semantic Feature Analysis

ENCOURAGING WRITING

- Discussion Web
- KWL-Plus—Know/Want to Learn/Learned
- Magnet Summaries
- Point of View Guides
- Possible Sentences
- Proposition/Support Outlines
- Pyramid Diagram
- RAFT—Role/Audience/Format/Topic

REPRESENTING INFORMATION GRAPHICALLY

- Analogy Graphic Organizer
- Concept Definition Mapping
- Different Perspectives
- Discussion Web
- Follow the Characters
- Frayer Model
- History Change Frame
- KWL-Plus—Know/Want to Learn/Learned
- Proposition/Support Outlines
- Pyramid Diagram
- Science Connection Overview
- Semantic Feature Analysis
- Story Mapping
- Structured Notetaking
- Test Strategy Outline
- Vocabulary Overview Guide

BUILDING STUDY SKILLS

- Follow the Characters
- History Change Frame
- Magnet Summaries
- Science Connection Overview
- Story Mapping
- Structured Notetaking
- Test Strategy Outline
- Whole Brain Memory Strategies

Strategies for Interactive Learning. Effective classroom teaching strategies involve students in a wide variety of interactive practices. Figure 1.2 categorizes the thirty teaching strategies highlighted in this book in terms of eight important student activities: *developing vocabulary, brainstorming of ideas, learning cooperatively, promoting discussion, interactive reading, encouraging writing, representing information graphically,* and *building study skills.* Note that a particular teaching strategy may include several of these student activities as integral components. Therefore, a teaching strategy may be cross-referenced in more than one of these student activity categories.

For example, the Discussion Web (page 43) is an excellent procedure for fostering discussion among students and it makes extensive use of cooperative learning activities. Students work to record pertinent information in a graphic outline, which can be subsequently used as a blueprint for various writing exercises. Finally, the Discussion Web involves students in a very directive and purposeful rereading of assigned material. Therefore, the Discussion Web strategy is indexed under five student activities: *learning cooperatively, promoting discussion, interactive reading, encouraging writing,* and *representing information graphically.*

Strategies That Stimulate Thinking. The classroom teaching strategies featured in this book are also categorized according to the kinds of thinking students will become involved in when engaged in the lesson. The cognitive behavior elicited by a strategy is

---

Effective strategies build in students a discipline for learning which enables them to become independent learners.

---

correlated to the three phases of instruction: (1) preparing students to encounter new content (before reading activities), (2) guiding students in their learning (during reading activities), and (3) enhancing or building upon the learning (after reading activities).

We want to encourage different types of thinking in students, depending on whether we are preparing them to learn new material, helping them to process while reading, or aiding them in consolidating new learning into their existing memory banks. Figure 1.3 identifies the cognitive mindset of strategic students during each phase of learning. Before reading, strategic learners **activate** what they know about the topic and they **focus** their attention on learning for a

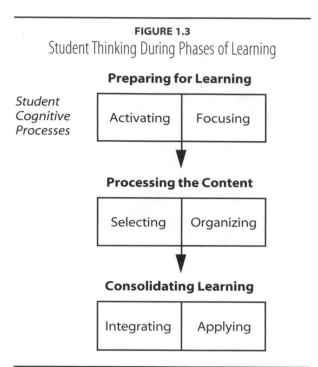

FIGURE 1.3
Student Thinking During Phases of Learning

Student Cognitive Processes

Preparing for Learning

| Activating | Focusing |

Processing the Content

| Selecting | Organizing |

Consolidating Learning

| Integrating | Applying |

specific purpose. During learning, strategic learners are actively engaged in **selecting** from the text what they deem is important to know, and they undertake some method to **organize** this information. And to consolidate their learning, strategic learners use strategies which help **integrate** the new information into what they already know. They also look for ways to **apply** this new information to meaningful situations.

As you use the classroom strategies described in this book, notice how they encourage the cognitive behaviors in Figure 1.4. For example, a frontloading strategy such as KWL-Plus (page 60) is an excellent way to prepare students for new learning because it encourages them to *activate* what they know and *focus* their attention on directions for new learning. A strategy such as Structured Notetaking (page 106) works with students because they are prompted to read *selectively* and to meaningfully *organize* important information. A RAFT writing exercise (page 87) helps students *integrate* new concepts into their previous understandings by having them personalize their learning. A RAFT assignment also provides students with a creative way to *apply* what they have learned.

Building Independent Learners. As teachers, we know that our students will not learn everything they will ever need to know in those thirteen years leading up to graduation from high school. In our daily work with students, we strive to cultivate people who will become lifelong learners, who will continue to deepen

FIGURE 1.4

Classroom Teaching Strategies Indexed by **Cognitive Processes**

PREPARING FOR LEARNING: ACTIVATING/FOCUSING STRATEGIES

Analogy Graphic Organizer
Anticipation Guides
Character Quotes
Concept Definition Mapping
Frayer Model
Guided Imagery
History Change Frame
KWL-Plus—Know/Want to Learn/Learned
LINK—List/Inquire/Note/Know
Possible Sentences
PReP—Prereading Plan
Problematic Situations
Science Connection Overview
Semantic Feature Analysis

PROCESSING THE CONTENT: SELECTING/ORGANIZING STRATEGIES

Analogy Graphic Organizer
Anticipation Guides
Character Quotes
Concept Definition Mapping
Frayer Model
History Change Frame
KWL-Plus—Know/Want to Learn/Learned
Point of View Guides
Possible Sentences
Problematic Situations
Proposition/Support Outlines
Pyramid Diagram
Science Connection Overview
Semantic Feature Analysis
SMART—Self-Monitoring Approach to Reading and Thinking
Story Mapping
Structured Notetaking

CONSOLIDATING LEARNING: INTEGRATING/APPLYING STRATEGIES

Analogy Graphic Organizer
Concept Definition Mapping
Different Perspectives
Discussion Web
Follow the Characters
Frayer Model
Guided Imagery
KWL-Plus—Know/Want to Learn/Learned
Magnet Summaries
Point of View Guides
Pyramid Diagram
RAFT—Role/Audience/Format/Topic
Save the Last Word for Me
Semantic Feature Analysis
SMART—Self-Monitoring Approach to Reading and Thinking)
Story Mapping
Structured Notetaking
Test Strategy Outline
Whole Brain Memory Strategies
Vocabulary Overview Guide

their understandings related to the various subject areas we teach. By using classroom strategies that teach students to activate, focus, select, organize, integrate, and apply as they learn, we will foster the development of individuals who are purposeful thinkers and independent learners. The classroom strategies outlined in this book should help your students understand, remember, and apply key information and concepts. But they are also designed to accomplish a gradual increase in student self-responsibility for learning. Effective strategies build in students a discipline for learning which enables them to become independent learners.

REFERENCES

Cook, D. (Ed.). (1986). *A guide to curriculum planning in reading.* Madison, WI: Wisconsin Department of Public Instruction.

Cook, D. (Ed.). (1989). *Strategic learning in the content areas.* Madison, WI: Wisconsin Department of Public Instruction.

CHAPTER 2

Guiding Thinking Through Text Frames

*I*t is a quiet evening. You are settled into a comfortable chair, anticipating a few hours pleasantly lost in the latest Tony Hillerman or P.D. James mystery. As you open the book to initially appraise it, what is your frame of mind? What are you expecting from this novel?

To put it another way, why did you choose a mystery to read this evening? Undoubtedly, it is because you were looking for the kind of reading experience that a mystery novel would satisfy. And your "frame of mind" is organized around a set of questions that a well-written mystery novel would be expected to answer. *What mystery in this book are we trying solve? What character in the book is searching for the solution? What clues can we identify? What false leads must we be wary of? Who are the suspects? What are their motives? What steps should we take to figure out this mystery?* You have the perfect frame of mind to approach the reading of this book.

Text Frames: A Mental Approach to Reading. Effective readers attack print with a very active, purposeful mindset. They know **why** they are reading a selection, and they know exactly **what** they are looking for. In other words, effective readers have an appropriate "frame of mind" that will structure how

---

Researchers use the term frame to describe these sets of questions that we expect to have answered in a specific piece of reading.

---

they read a particular piece of writing. In essence, they read to answer a set of relevant questions about the material—questions that relate directly to their purpose for reading that material in the first place.

Researchers use the term *frame* to describe these sets of questions that we expect to have answered in a specific piece of reading (Anderson and Armbruster, 1984). For example, those questions outlining what to look for in a mystery novel could be collectively termed a *mystery frame*. We have all internalized this mystery frame, which guides us as we read and enables us to organize what we read so that the story make sense. Our mystery "frame of mind" prompts us

to automatically look for clues and suspects, motives and alibis.

Frames provide a sense of structure; they outline boundaries and delineate shape. For example, eyeglasses' frames, picture frames, and window frames all serve to hold something together into a certain shape and form. Likewise, the legal term "to be framed" implies that the pattern of evidence has been arranged so that an innocent person is defined as being guilty. Frames used by authors, then, provide a sense of coherence to the writing. By considering what questions the writing needs to answer, authors have a blueprint that guides them into selecting the most appropriate information for inclusion in the text and they have a clear scheme for organizing this information. Authors write according to various frames.

Examples of Common Frames. It is easy to identify the questions that make up a mystery frame, and most of our students would have no difficulty describing what they should look for in a mystery story or novel. But how about the kind of writing that students encounter in their textbooks? What frame of mind should a student assume when reading a biology passage on microorganisms, for example? What questions should students seek to answer in a health section on smoking? Or in a social studies chapter on the Roman Empire? What text frames are represented in these materials?

Jones, Palincsar, Ogle, and Carr (1987) highlight a number of text frames that authors use to organize different types of information. Common frames include compare/contrast, concept/definition, cause/effect, problem/solution, proposition/support, and goal/action/outcome. Each of these text frames signals the most effective way to approach the reading of a specific piece of material. A United States history passage on the Great Depression might be most successfully read from a problem/solution frame of mind. A section of the Chemistry textbook might follow a cause/effect frame. A newspaper editorial used during language arts instruction would probably follow a proposition/support frame. A Geometry chapter on characteristics of different triangles may require a compare/contrast orientation. Figure 2.1 highlights the questions implied in these six most common text frames.

FIGURE 2.1
Determining Text Frames—What is the point of the material?

1. **That a problem needs solving?** *(Problem/Solution Frame)*

   - What is the problem?
   - Who has the problem?
   - What is causing the problem?
   - What are the effects of the problem?
   - Who is trying to solve the problem?
   - What solutions are recommended or attempted?
   - What results from these solutions?
   - Is the problem solved? Do any new problems develop because of the solutions?

2. **That certain things result from certain conditions?** *(Cause/Effect Frame)*

   - What is it that happens?
   - What causes it to happen?
   - What are the important elements or factors that cause this effect?
   - How do these factors or elements interrelate?
   - Will this result always happen from these causes? Why or why not?
   - How would the result change if the elements or factors are different?

3. **That certain things are similar, or different?** *(Compare/Contrast Frame)*

   - What is being compared and contrasted?
   - What categories of characteristics or attributes are used to compare and contrast these things?
   - How are the things alike or similar?
   - How are the things not alike or different?
   - What are the most important qualities or attributes that make them similar?
   - What are the most important qualities or attributes that make them different?
   - In terms of the qualities that are most important, are these things more alike, or more different?
   - What can we conclude about these things or items?

4. **That people are trying to do something for a specific reason?** *(Goal/Action/Outcome Frame)*

   - Who are the people involved?
   - What are they trying to do or achieve? What is their goal?
   - What actions do they take to achieve their goal?
   - What are the effects of their actions? What happens?
   - Were these actions successful for achieving their goal?
   - Are there unexpected outcomes from their actions?
   - Would other actions have been more effective? Could they have done something else?

5. **That a concept needs to be understood?** *(Concept/Definition Frame)*

   - What is the concept?
   - To what category does it belong?
   - What are its critical characteristics or attributes?
   - How does it work?
   - What does it do?
   - What are its functions?
   - What are examples of it?
   - What are examples of things that share some but not all of its characteristics?

6. **That a viewpoint is being argued and supported?** *(Proposition/Support Frame)*

   - What is the general topic area or issue?
   - What proposition (viewpoint, theory, hypothesis, thesis) is being presented?
   - How is this proposition supported?
   - Are examples provided? Do the examples support the proposition?
   - Are data provided? Does the data support the proposition?
   - Is expert verification provided? Does it support the proposition?
   - Is a logical argument provided? Does it support the proposition?
   - Is a sufficient case presented to warrant acceptance of the proposition?

Thinking about a text frame during reading helps students become more directive and purposeful in their learning. The frame establishes their "attitude" toward the assignment. Obviously their "attitude" while reading a mystery is to think like a detective. Their "attitude" when immersed in problem/solution relationships might be described as that of a "troubleshooter"—someone who examines what is wrong, why it is wrong, and how we can fix it. (See Figure 2.2: Metaphors for Text Frames.) A cause/effect text frame invites students to think like a "scientist," asking what happens and why it happens. Students reading concept/definition material might think like a "news reporter," asking who, what, where, when, and how questions. Students might adopt a "shopper's" mind-

---

A text frame *frames* the most important arguments or information in a piece of writing so that the reader "gets the point."

---

set when grappling with compare/contrast material, weighing how products are alike and different. Students might best approach proposition/support writing like a "judge," who analyzes arguments and evaluates the strength of corroborating "evidence." Finally, a "team sports coach" perspective might get students into the right frame of mind for reading goal/action/outcome material. A coach works to identify the actions the players need to take to meet the team's goals, and then evaluates these actions in terms of the results of the season.

Strategies That "Frame" Instruction. A text frame, then, *frames* the most important arguments or information in a piece of writing so that the reader "gets the point" and can make some sense of it. So how can we get students to read with an active *frame of mind* when they tackle textbook and other print material we use in our classrooms? The answer lies in the teaching strategies we use when involving our students in reading assignments. We can use strategies that "tip off" students to the appropriate frame for reading.

For example, suppose your students are going to read a passage about snowshoe hares. Determine first what text "frame of mind" you want them to slip into. If the passage emphasizes problems the snowshoe hare is encountering in today's world, work your strategy around *problem/solution* questions. If the passage describes similarities and differences between

FIGURE 2.2

Metaphors for Text Frames

Problem/Solution — a Troubleshooter
Cause/Effect — a Scientist
Compare/Contrast — a Shopper
Proposition/Support — a Judge
Goal/Action/Outcome — a Team Sports Coach
Concept/Definition — a News Reporter

the hare and various types of rabbits, structure the assignment around *compare/contrast* questions. If the reasons why hares are returning to some regions are discussed, work around a *cause/effect* frame. If the author is presenting a theory as to why the hares have survived but other species haven't, stress *proposition/support* relationships. If the article is about the Sierra Club's efforts to save the hare, then *goal/action/outcome* is the natural structure for the assignment. If the passage is a general informational segment on what snowshoe hares are, where they live, and what they do, *concept/definition* questions should predominate.

The teaching strategies presented in this book can be effectively used to signal text frame to students. Using these strategies with students can provide the support they need in order to read in the "right" frame of mind. Figure 2.3 relates the thirty strategies highlighted in Section 2 with these six common text frames.

REFERENCES

Anderson, T., & Armbruster, B. (1984). Studying. In P.D. Pearson (Ed.), *Handbook of reading research*. New York: Longman.

Buehl, D. (1991). Frames of mind. *The Exchange. Secondary Reading Interest Group Newsletter, 4*(2).

Jones, B., Palincsar, A., Ogle, D., & Carr, E. (1987). *Strategic teaching and learning: Cognitive instruction in the content areas.* Alexandria, VA: ASCD.

FIGURE 2.3
Classroom Teaching Strategies Indexed by **Text Frames**

CAUSE/EFFECT
Anticipation Guides
Follow the Characters
History Change Frame
Problematic Situations
RAFT—Role/Audience/Format/Topic
Science Connection Overview
Structured Notetaking

CONCEPT/DEFINITION
Analogy Graphic Organizer
Concept/Definition Mapping
Frayer Model
Guided Imagery
LINK—List/Inquire/Note/Know
Magnet Summaries
Possible Sentences
PReP (Prereading Plan)
Pyramid Diagram
RAFT—Role/Audience/Format/Topic
Science Connection Overview
Semantic Feature Analysis
Structured Notetaking
Vocabulary Overview Guide

PROBLEM/SOLUTION
Anticipation Guides
History Change Frame
Problematic Situations
RAFT—Role/Audience/Format/Topic
SMART—Self-Monitoring Approach
  to Reading and Thinking
Structured Notetaking
Test Strategy Outline

COMPARE/CONTRAST
Analogy Graphic Organizer
Different Perspectives
Discussion Web
Frayer Model
History Change Frame
Pyramid Diagram
RAFT—Role/Audience/Format/Topic
Semantic Feature Analysis
Structured Notetaking

PROPOSITION/SUPPORT
Anticipation Guides
Character Quotes
Discussion Web
Point of View Guide
Proposition/Support Outline
RAFT—Role/Audience/Format/Topic
Save the Last Word for Me
Structured Notetaking

GOAL/ACTION/OUTCOME
History Change Frame
RAFT—Role/Audience/Format/Topic
SMART—Self-Monitoring Approach
  to Reading and Thinking
Story Mapping
Structured Notetaking
Test Strategy Outline
Whole Brain Memory Strategies

CHAPTER 3

Setting Priorities With Fact Pyramids

"If you remember only one thing about this, it ought to be..."

For many of our students, the remembering of one thing about a unit, a chapter, or a lesson would be a tall order. Unfortunately, many students seem to conceptualize learning in school as a short-term process. They see their classes only as a steady barrage of information, and they cope by trying to remember only long enough to pass a test. Then it's on to the next material. Teachers find it discouraging that so many of our students seem to retain so little of what they supposedly "learned" in school?

Of course, we also realize that "losing" some of what we've learned is a natural process. Each one of us can think of personal examples of this "selective forgetting." We have all experienced those moments when we have to admit to a student (or a son or daughter) that we cannot recall enough to help him or her with the homework for another teacher's class. Hopefully we have retained the central concepts of the material, but like most people, we have forgotten much of the specific detail.

The Forest and Acres and Acres of Trees. One reason students seem so readily disposed to quickly forget much of the information they encounter in school is due to the nature of the material itself. We want students to be able to differentiate and prioritize as they process material. We want them continually making determinations as to what is most important and worthy of knowing over time. But often our textbooks make "selective processing" a challenging task for students. In a recent analysis, Kennedy (1991) criticizes textbooks for burying "big ideas"—those most worthy of being remembered—underneath a tremendous array of what she terms "factlets." Textbooks are often poorly organized and do not satisfactorily cue students as to how to maneuver through all the factual information so that it makes sense. Textbooks tend to be written to *expose* students to information rather than to help them truly understand it.

Thus, "school" for many students is construed as an overwhelming load of factual information which never gets sorted out into something useful and worth remembering. The old adage that they "can't see the

forest for the trees" becomes a daily occurrence for students immersed in the factual detail of their textbooks. As a consequence, activities that help students "see the point" of new material are especially important. Questions which guide students into sorting through factual information and making meaningful connections will more likely lead to the kind of long-term associations that makes learning memorable.

Unfortunately, this primary means of guiding students through new information—the asking of questions—often does not help students with their learning. Klein (1988) summarizes the research on

---

Textbooks tend to be written to *expose* students to information rather than to help them truly understand it.

---

student questions and reports that few of these questions are actually designed to *assist* students as they learn. Most questions merely *assess* whether students learned. Klein also notes that most questions are asked after rather than during reading, and that questions predominately target a literal level of understanding. Furthermore, most questions could be answered with a rote, paraphrase-level of processing, and often with only a single word or short phrase. Finally, most questions, especially those that appear in textbooks, have no clear and coherent focus. It's as if some of them were written at random, and students come to assume that anything that appears on a page of text is fair game for a question, whether it is truly important or not.

World Brains and School Brains. As a result, many students operate in school as if they possessed not one, but two brains. These two brains do not correspond with the familiar right hemisphere/left hemisphere dichotomy. Instead, imagine the mind split into a *World Brain* and a *School Brain*. The World Brain can be visualized as taking up most of the room in the student's skull. In it are stored all of what the student knows and understands about the world, all of life's experiences and personal explanations of "what is" and "why" and "how." The student relies on this World Brain to make sense of the world. In

Chapter 1 we referred to the World Brain as the student's background knowledge.

Now imagine the School Brain, located in an out-of-the-way corner of the mind and occupying only a small cavity. Think of the School Brain as carefully insulated from the World Brain—very little that enters it ever gets transferred into the brain that

---

Imagine the following scenario: five years from now, as you walk along the street, you meet one of the students you are currently teaching. What should this person still remember from your class?

---

makes sense of things. The School Brain has a minuscule storage capacity, but that is quite all right—information does not need to stay there very long. The most distinctive feature of the School Brain is a ever-open chute, ready to dump yesterday's lesson quickly and irrevocably into oblivion. Students use the School Brain for short-term storage of the daily stuff of school; as soon as the test is over, or a new chapter started, they flush out the backlog of old facts and stray information and ready themselves for another cycle of short-term learning. Nothing stays around very long in the School Brain.

Certainly some of our students are very adept at perceiving the connections between what they already know and understand and what they are learning in our classrooms. They are able to successfully integrate new information into their existing mental structures, and they find that the new information does indeed help them to make more sense of their world. But for many of our students, school has little to do with the real world, and their failure to make connections virtually insures that much of what they learn in school will be lost—relegated to the dead-end depot of the School Brain.

Prioritizing Factual Information. How can student activities be structured so that real learning takes place, so that a true conceptual change occurs in the mind, so that important information is retained over time and not merely long enough to pass tests? Classroom strategies which guide students into making connections between their background knowledge (the World Brain) and what they are studying in class (the School Brain) will increase the probability that the new information will find a place in long-term memory.

Imagine the following scenario: five years from now, as you walk along the street, you meet one of the students you are currently teaching. What should this person still remember from your class? You know that much of the specific information the student had encountered will be forgotten. But what has to still be there, or you'll be bitterly disappointed? What does this former student need to remember about the New Deal, or cell division, or congruent triangles, or *To Kill a Mockingbird*? To ask it in another way, did this former student "get the point" from these various units of instruction?

It is unlikely that you would be crestfallen if your former student could not name the provisions of National Industrial Recovery Act or identify Henry Wallace, as long as he or she recognized the New Deal as an extensive governmental reaction to the Great Depression that included support for American citizens. Likewise, you probably would not expect your former student to name the various stages of mitosis, or recall specific theorems. You would, however, expect a basic understanding that cells divide as an explanation of growth of living organisms and you would hope for an internalization of the basic principles of triangles, such as the relationship between angles.

Essentially, then, you would concede that some factual information will in all likelihood be forgotten over time, but that other, more transcendent, information must be remembered if one is to be regarded as a literate person. Fact Pyramids (Buehl, 1991) provide teachers with a structured way of analyzing information so that our teaching will guide students' focus toward big ideas—those few facts and concepts that we truly want students to remember over time. Fact Pyramids graphically categorize text information into three levels: (1) essential facts; (2) short-term facts; and (3) supportive detail (see Figure 3.1).

FIGURE 3.1

Fact Pyramid

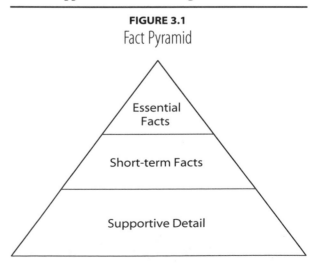

Essential facts are those concepts or ideas that one would expect a literate person to know over time. If you remember only one thing about a lesson or unit, this is it. Essential facts are still with us five years later. They represent the "point" of the lesson.

Short-term facts comprise the necessary information that allows concepts to be learned with some level of sophistication, but they will generally be forgotten over time. These facts make up much of the language of class discussion and instruction, the key vocabulary and major details, but ultimately they are not important as ends in themselves. Students use short-term facts to construct a deeper understanding of a concept or idea.

Supportive detail represents the more specific information which provides the depth to flesh out an understanding but which does not need to be learned for its own sake. Certainly a rich text supplies the reader with more than "headlines" and "boldface vocabulary." Supportive detail comprises the "semantic glue" for a text, the elaborations and examples that help to illuminate understanding. Supportive detail can be an asset in textbooks, but such information should not be emphasized as "factlets" that draw students' attention away from central ideas.

Integrating Fact Pyramids Into Your Teaching.
Using the concept of Fact Pyramids can help teachers make decisions about which teaching strategies can best differentiate among the types of information delivered in a chapter. By categorizing information in terms of these three levels, teachers can identify shortcomings with a textbook's organization and questions. Are the elements of the text that you regard as essential readily apparent to your students? Or will your students have to "dig" for them? Will students become overwhelmed by the factual information and cope by completing answers to questions without ever really realizing the "point" of the material? Will students be able to learn the "essentials" without losing their way through the factual information.

The questions for student learning provided in textbooks are typically guilty of diverting student attention away from essential concepts. Unfortunately, many textbook questions ask students to focus on supportive detail information. For example, the following question in a United States History textbook involves students in processing supportive detail to complete the assignment:

Identify the following: (a) Benjamin Wade, (b) Henry Davis, (c) John Wilkes Booth,

(d) Thaddeus Stevens, and (e) Charles Sumner.

Such a question sends a wrong message to students. First, they are led to believe that because a name was mentioned in the text, it is worthy of attention. John Wilkes Booth, the assassin of Abraham Lincoln, is well-known, but most literate adults would not be able to identify the other people on this list. Second, all of the above people are treated as equally important. Students are given no direction in evaluating which information is most deserving of attention. Third, students know they will forget these people within a short period of time, and they begin to regard all information that they encounter in history, for example, as equally forgettable.

Instead, a Fact Pyramid constructed for the post Civil War period might help clarify which text information is actually worth asking students to write about (see Figure 3.2). A history teacher might decide on

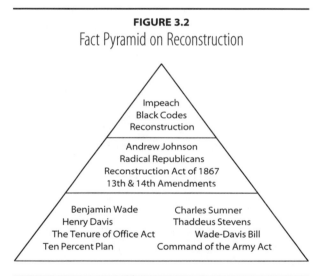

FIGURE 3.2
Fact Pyramid on Reconstruction

the following essential facts for this period of study: "Reconstruction was a federal government action to monitor bringing the Southern states back into the union," "black codes were passed to deny the newly freed slaves their rights," and "disagreements over Reconstruction led to the impeachment of a President." This information should receive primary focus in text questions.

Short-term facts for this unit might include the major players in this controversy, President Andrew Johnson and the Radical Republicans. The major provisions of the Reconstruction Act of 1867 will probably become hazy for most students over time, but a sense that the federal government controlled the Southern states (through use of troops) will perhaps remain.

Although many students will forget which amendment did what; most should realize that Constitutional amendments abolished slavery and guaranteed "due process."

Finally, specific information about people such as Benjamin Wade or Charles Sumner, or pieces of legislation such as the Tenure of Office Act, represent supportive detail useful only to broaden and enrich the understanding of major ideas of this unit. Few adults would be able to successfully identify most of this information. Direct questions on supportive detail information should thus be avoided.

A fact pyramid created for a Health textbook chapter on "Nutrition" is featured in Figure 3.3. This chapter contains a great deal of detailed information

---

FIGURE 3.3
Fact Pyramid on Nutrition

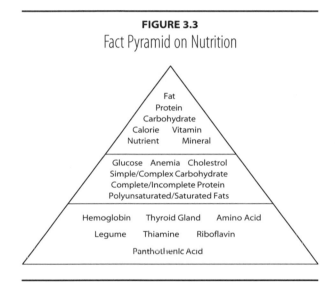

---

on the six nutrients found in food and is packed with biology-type terminology that would be hard for most of the students to wade through. What would a Health teacher expect a former student to *still* know about this material five years later? Clearly it could be conceded that much of the material would very likely be forgotten. Certainly the fact that complex carbohydrates consist of long chains of glucose is known by very few adults. Few Health teachers would realistically expect a former student to remember the differences between fat-soluble and water-soluble vitamins. Specific facts about amino acids are also not likely to last over time.

Three priorities perhaps emerge from this material. First, there is a connection between what you eat and how your body functions. Second, different nutrients supply different important ingredients to a healthy diet. Third, specific nutrients are found in a variety of different foods. *Essential facts,* then, could include the six nutrients (fats, proteins, carbohydrates,

minerals, vitamins, and water) and the contribution of each to a healthy diet. "Calorie" is a frequently used concept, so students should also have a meaningful connection to that term. This is the material students should know over time.

The *short-term facts* include more specific information related to the nutrients. These facts play a role in the discussion of nutrition, but they do not need to be learned as information for its own sake. Many adults are probably murky on the differences between simple and complex carbohydrates, complete and incomplete proteins, and polyunsaturated and saturated fats.

Most of this Health chapter is made up of *supportive details,* many of which are difficult to understand. Information related to terms such as hemoglobin, panthothenic acid, enzyme activities, the thyroid gland and so forth is too specific to warrant student attention. Most students would have insufficient background to adequately absorb such information. An emphasis on learning these details distracts students from the overall point of the material.

Fact Pyramids are constructed by teachers to spotlight what is important and worthy of being remembered over time. They allow teachers to adapt their textbooks and target questions which do help students be selective and get the point (the "tip" of the pyramid). They lead to using teaching strategies that engage students in successfully handling material that contains a wealth of detail.

REFERENCES

Buehl, D. (May, 1991). Fact pyramids. *New perspectives: Reading across the curriculum.* Madison, WI: Madison Metropolitan School District.

Kennedy, M. (May, 1991). Policy issues in teacher education. *Phi Delta Kappan.*

Klein, M. (1988). *Teaching reading comprehension and vocabulary: A guide for teachers.* Englewood Cliffs, NJ: Prentice Hall.

Classroom Strategies for Teaching and Learning

Matching Strategies to Your Instruction

When is the best time to use one of the class-room teaching strategies described in this section? Each classroom strategy will be introduced by an index in the lower right corner to help identify the strengths of the strategy in terms of cognitive processes, text frame, and student activities. (See the index example below.)

Cognitive processes refer to the kinds of thinking that students will be engaged in during instruction. As discussed in Chapter 1, strategies which prepare students to learn are ones that *activate* background knowledge and *focus* attention on important concepts. Strategies which help students during reading involve the *selecting* and *organizing* of information. Strategies which work to consolidate learning after reading include exercises which help students *integrate* new learning into their memories and *apply* it to some useful context.

Text frame refers to the way thinking is organized during reading and learning activities. Chapter 2 outlined the six basic text frames that condition a student's "frame of mind" during the lesson: *cause/effect, concept/definition, problem/solution, compare/contrast, proposition/support,* and *goal/action/outcome.* Text frames help students ask themselves the right questions about the material as they learn.

Student activities refer to the various ways a classroom strategy can involve students in learning. Chapter 1 detailed eight student activities that connect to instructional goals for students during their learning: *developing vocabulary, brainstorming of ideas, learning cooperatively, promoting discussion, interactive reading, encouraging writing, representing information graphically,* and *building study skills.*

The strategy index which appears in the lower right corner to introduce each strategy is divided into cognitive processes, text frame, and student activity. For each strategy, certain items in each category are highlighted. These items represent those cognitive processes, text frames, and student activities most emphasized by the strategy. Notice that several strategies emphasize more than one cognitive process, text

frame, or student activity. Use the strategy index in your instructional planning as a guide for identifying the particular strengths of each classroom strategy.

For example, the first classroom strategy in this section is the Analogy Graphic Organizer (opposite page). The strategy index has all six cognitive process highlighted, because the Analogy Graphic Organizer can be used before, during, and after reading with students. The two text frames which are highlighted, *concept/definition* and *compare/contrast,* indicate that the Analogy Graphic Organizer involves students in developing understanding of concepts and includes activities which stimulate students to make compare and contrast decisions. Four student activities are highlighted, which indicate that the Analogy Graphic Organizer is a strategy that develops vocabulary, engages students in brainstorming from their background knowledge, promotes discussion among students, and includes procedures that involve students in creating graphic representations of information.

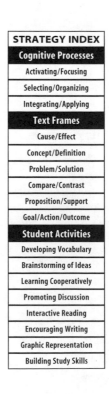

STRATEGY INDEX
Cognitive Processes
Activating/Focusing
Selecting/Organizing
Integrating/Applying
Text Frames
Cause/Effect
Concept/Definition
Problem/Solution
Compare/Contrast
Proposition/Support
Goal/Action/Outcome
Student Activities
Developing Vocabulary
Brainstorming of Ideas
Learning Cooperatively
Promoting Discussion
Interactive Reading
Encouraging Writing
Graphic Representation
Building Study Skills

Analogy Graphic Organizer

"You mean it's *like*...?" The eyes light up. The concept you are teaching comes alive. An analogy that relates to your students' lives has helped them make a connection.

Teachers know that analogies are a powerful way to help students understand new information or concepts. "Cells are the building blocks of your body *like* bricks are the building blocks of this school." "The judicial branch of government is *like* the umpires in baseball." "A poem written in iambic pentameter is

---

Analogies are a powerful way to help students understand new information or concepts.

---

like a dance that has five steps." Analogies help students link new information to familiar concepts.

The Analogy Graphic Organizer (Buehl and Hein, 1990) is a strategy that provides a visual framework for students to analyze key relationships in an analogy. The compare/contrast structure serves to broaden their understanding of important concepts or vocabulary. An Analogy Graphic Organizer can be used with students to introduce a topic, to guide comprehension while reading, or to extend the learning after reading.

THE STRATEGY

Analogy Graphic Organizers help students use an analogy to perceive the similarities and differences between a new concept and something familiar to their lives. Using this strategy involves the following steps:

1 Determine what students know about possible analogous relationships that involve the concept being introduced. Select one familiar concept to help the students develop analogous relationships to the new concept. For example, students studying the concept "colony" in a history class could relate to a situation with which they are very familiar—being a dependent child in a family.

2 Introduce the Analogy Graphic Organizer on an overhead transparency (see "Colony" example). Brainstorm with students the specific characteristics or properties that may be common between the two concepts. Enter these in the column marked "Similarities." Students might offer that a colony and being a child in a family share the following characteristics: both are dependent for many of their needs on the "parents," both have to follow rules set by others, both are related to the "parents," and both sometimes feel resentment and eventually want to be independent.

3 Next ask the students to generate how the two concepts are not alike, and write these in the "Differences" column. Initially, steps 2 and 3 will need to be modeled by the teacher, but after students develop more independence, individual copies of a blank Analogy Graphic Organizer can be given to students to complete in cooperative groups.

In our Colony example, students may notice that a colony is usually geographically separate from its "mother country," while a child usually lives with the other members of the family. They may also recall that a Colony is regarded as a negative system today, while families are not. And a Colony's move toward independence has often been associated with violence, not a characteristic of most families.

4 Discuss with students the categories that make up the basis for the comparison. Some of the similarities (both colonies and children rely on the "parent" for protection and other basic needs; both are at an earlier stage of development) might be labeled as *Dependence on Others*. Other similarities might be categorized under *Kinship or Family Background* and *Control/Self-Determination*.

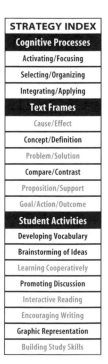

STRATEGY INDEX
Cognitive Processes
Activating/Focusing
Selecting/Organizing
Integrating/Applying
Text Frames
Cause/Effect
Concept/Definition
Problem/Solution
Compare/Contrast
Proposition/Support
Goal/Action/Outcome
Student Activities
Developing Vocabulary
Brainstorming of Ideas
Learning Cooperatively
Promoting Discussion
Interactive Reading
Encouraging Writing
Graphic Representation
Building Study Skills

Analogy Graphic Organizer

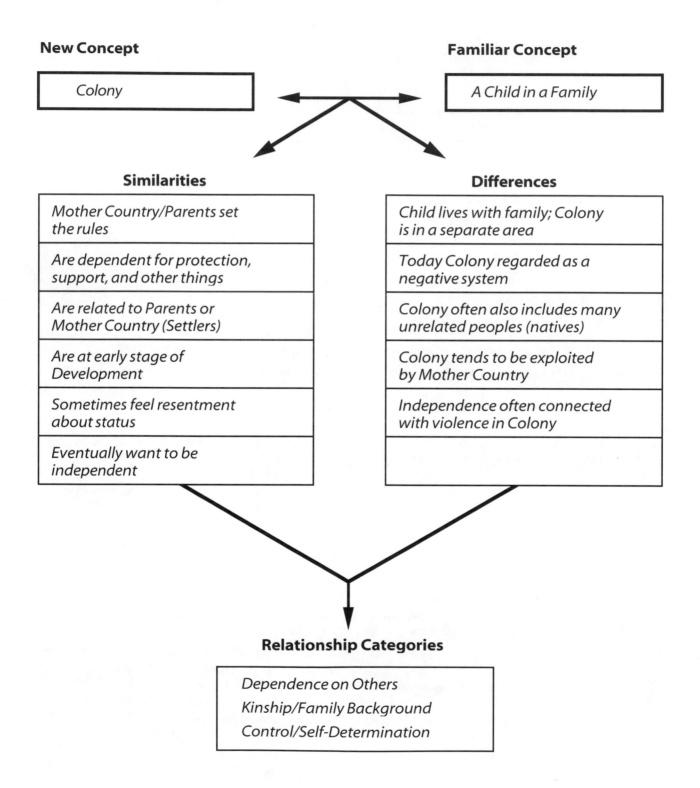

New Concept

Colony

Familiar Concept

A Child in a Family

Similarities

Mother Country/Parents set the rules
Are dependent for protection, support, and other things
Are related to Parents or Mother Country (Settlers)
Are at early stage of Development
Sometimes feel resentment about status
Eventually want to be independent

Differences

Child lives with family; Colony is in a separate area
Today Colony regarded as a negative system
Colony often also includes many unrelated peoples (natives)
Colony tends to be exploited by Mother Country
Independence often connected with violence in Colony

Relationship Categories

Dependence on Others Kinship/Family Background Control/Self-Determination

5 Students are now prepared to use the Analogy Graphic Organizer to write a summary of how the new concept and familiar concept are alike. Students may come to see that, like children, colonies often depend a great deal on their parent, but that eventually colonies "grow up" and want to assume self-control over their lives. Colonies, however, may feel exploited, and resentments may lead to violence in the process of gaining independence.

ADVANTAGES

Analogy Graphic Organizers offer a number of advantages for use with students:

- Students enhance their understanding of new concepts or vocabulary through the analysis of familiar analogous concepts.

- Students make connections to new material by activating related experiences and background.

- Students gain practice in writing well-organized summaries that follow a compare/contrast structure.

- This strategy can be adapted for use from elementary through secondary levels, and is appropriate for all content areas.

FURTHER RESOURCES

Buehl, D., & Hein, D. (1990). Analogy graphic organizer. *The Exchange. Secondary Reading Interest Group Newsletter,* 3(2).

Cook, D., (Ed.). (1989). *Strategic learning in the content areas,* Madison, WI: Department of Public Instruction.

Anticipation Guides

Suppose you are going out this evening for dinner at a gourmet restaurant. As you anticipate the evening, which of the following statements reflect what you might be expecting? "Gourmet meals are very expensive." "Gourmet meals feature foods that are difficult to prepare at home." "Gourmet dining is a relaxed and very pleasurable experience." "Gourmet meals feature small portions." "Gourmet foods are delicious but fattening." After dinner, as you drive home from the restaurant, you will probably be thinking about whether your experience was consistent with what you had anticipated.

Students respond to statements which challenge or support their preconceived ideas.

The Anticipation Guide (Herber, 1978) is a strategy that forecasts the major ideas of a passage through the use of statements that activate students' thoughts and opinions. Before reading a selection, students respond to several statements which challenge or support their preconceived ideas related to key concepts in the passage. Students then have an opportunity to explain or elaborate upon their responses in small group or class discussion. This process arouses interest, sets purposes for reading, and encourages higher level thinking—all important aspects of pre-reading motivation. The Anticipation Guide can then be used when students have completed their reading to evaluate how well the material has been understood and to insure that misconceptions have been corrected.

THE STRATEGY

Anticipation Guides can be used in almost any learning situation in any content area, and they are effective with nonprint media as well as with written materials. Using this strategy involves the following steps:

1 Identify the major ideas and concepts in the text the students will be reading. For example, students studying acid rain in a science class may need to focus their attention on the following ideas as they read:

- Acid rain has a harmful effect on aquatic life.

- Acid rain also destroys bridges, buildings, and statues.

- There are multiple causes of acid rain, including auto and factory emissions.

- Stopping acid rain involves economic trade-offs.

- Acid rain problems are increasing in Wisconsin.

2 Next, consider your students' experiences and beliefs that will be either supported or challenged by the reading. Decide what your students probably already know about the topic or ideas to be covered. This step insures that students will be able to offer responses to an Anticipation Guide about the reading.

In our science example, most students will have heard of acid rain and probably realize that it has a negative effect on our lakes. Some may have opinions about its impact of Wisconsin. Some students will also probably know that acid rain is connected to the burning of fossil fuels, and that controlling it is controversial.

3 Create an Anticipation Guide of three to six statements that challenge or modify your students' preexisting understandings of the material. Include some statements which will elicit agreement between the students and the information in the text. The most effective statements are those about which students have

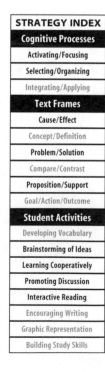

STRATEGY INDEX

Cognitive Processes
Activating/Focusing
Selecting/Organizing
Integrating/Applying

Text Frames
Cause/Effect
Concept/Definition
Problem/Solution
Compare/Contrast
Proposition/Support
Goal/Action/Outcome

Student Activities
Developing Vocabulary
Brainstorming of Ideas
Learning Cooperatively
Promoting Discussion
Interactive Reading
Encouraging Writing
Graphic Representation
Building Study Skills

Anticipation Guide
(Science Example)

"Acid Rain"

Directions: Each of the following statements concern problems associated with acid rain.

• Put a check next to any statement with which you **agree**.

• Be prepared to support your views on **each statement** by thinking about what you know about acid rain and its effects. You will be sharing this information with other members of your group when you discuss these six statements.

_____ 1. Acid Rain kills fish.

_____ 2. The major cause of acid rain is fuel emissions from automobiles.

_____ 3. Stopping acid rain will cause some people to lose their jobs.

_____ 4. Acid rain problems are not yet serious in Wisconsin.

_____ 5. Acid rain is made up of sulfur oxides.

_____ 6. If acid rain is not controlled, we will experience a major environmental disaster.

Anticipation Guide
(Literature Example)

"Call of the Wild"

Directions: In the column labeled **<u>you</u>**, place a check next to any statement with which you tend to **agree**. Be prepared to support your opinions with examples.

After reading the book *Call of the Wild*, you will be comparing your opinions on these statements with those of the author, Jack London. Then you will check those statements that you feel **<u>Jack London</u>** would agree with.

	Jack	
You	London	

_____ _____ 1. Only the strong survive in this world.

_____ _____ 2. People must live in harmony with their environment.

_____ _____ 3. Greed makes people cruel.

_____ _____ 4. The primitive instinct exists in all people.

_____ _____ 5. Much of what happens to people is the result of fate.

_____ _____ 6. People will adapt to their surroundings in order to survive.

— Sarah Conroy (1993)

some knowledge but do not necessarily have a complete understanding. (See Science "Acid Rain" Anticipation Guide.)

In a literature class, to prepare students for thinking about some of the major themes of the novel *The Call of the Wild,* an Anticipation Guide could offer statements which elicit student opinions on some of the ideas explored by the author. (See Literature "Call of the Wild" Anticipation Guide.)

4 Present the Guide on the chalkboard, an overhead projector, or as individual student handouts. Leave space on the left for individual or small group response. As each statement is discussed, students must provide justification for their opinions. You may wish to have students first fill out the guide individually and then defend their responses to others in small groups or within a class discussion. Another variation is to have the students rank order the statements in terms of which they agree with the most to the least.

5 The students are now ready to read the selection. Ask the students to focus upon the information in the reading that confirms, elaborates, or rejects each of the statements in the Anticipation Guide. If students are reading material that can be marked, instruct them to underline or highlight the sections that are germane to each statement as they read.

Anticipation Guides are excellent ways to introduce nonprint media such as videos and films.

---

6 After completing the reading, students return to the statements in the Anticipation Guide to determine whether they have changed their minds regarding any of them. In cooperative groups, have them locate the information from the text which supports or rejects each statement. Students then rewrite any statement that needs to be altered based on the selection they have read.

Another option is to include in the Anticipation Guide two columns for responses—for the students and for the author. After reading the passage, students then compare their opinions on each statement with those of the author. This is especially effective for responding to ideas presented in literature. (See "Call of the Wild" example.)

ADVANTAGES

Anticipation Guides facilitate student learning in a number of respects:

- Students are cued into the major ideas of a selection *before* they start reading.

- Students activate some of what they know about the information before they read, and they are able to share their background knowledge with their classmates.

- Students become motivated to read in order to determine whether the text will confirm their opinions and ideas. They are also eager to read to disprove their classmates.

- Student misconceptions about a topic are addressed openly and are more likely to be changed after reading and discussing the new material.

- This strategy can be modified and used successfully with students from elementary age to high school. Anticipation Guides may be developed in all content areas and are excellent ways to introduce nonprint media such as videos and films as well as for preparing students to read.

FURTHER RESOURCES

Herber, H. (1978). *Teaching reading in content areas* (2nd ed.). Englewood Cliffs, NJ: Prentice-Hall, Inc.

Readence, J., Bean, T., & Baldwin, R. (1989). *Content area reading: An integrated approach* (3rd ed.). Dubuque, IA: Kendall/Hunt Publishing Company.

Character Quotes

""*Give me liberty or give me death!" "Ask not what your country can do for you, ask what you can do for your country." "We have nothing to fear but fear itself." "With malice toward none, with charity for all." "I have a dream that one day this nation will rise up and live out the true meaning of its creeds—'we hold these truths to be self-evident that all men are created equal.' "*

*"I'm the most terrific liar you ever saw in your life. It's awful." "One of my troubles is, I never care too much when I lose something—it used to drive my mother crazy when I was a kid." "I hate fist fights. I don't mind getting hit so much—although I'm not crazy about it, naturally—but what scares me most in a fist fight is the guy's face." "It was one of the worst schools I ever went to. It was full of phonies. And mean guys. You never saw so many mean guys in your life." "Just because somebody's dead, you don't just stop liking them, for God's sake—especially if they were about a thousand times nicer than the people you know that're **alive** and all."*

The power of expressive language! From the stirring rhetoric of past political leaders in the first paragraph to the introspective musings of Holden Caulfield in Salinger's *Catcher in the Rye* in the

---

Character Quotes is a strategy that can be used to introduce characters in fictional literature, or it can be used to elicit discussions of real life individuals.

---

second, spoken words have been a significant way people reveal themselves to others. Character Quotes (adapted from Blachowicz, 1993) is a strategy that helps students develop insights into character analysis through what a person says. The strategy involves the examination of representative quotes by a person as a way to develop a more sophisticated understanding of that person.

THE STRATEGY

Character Quotes is a strategy that can be used to introduce characters in fictional literature, or it can be used to elicit discussions of real life individuals, such as with social studies materials. The strategy follows these steps:

1 Preview the story or novel to identify several quotes by a character which illustrate different elements of the character's personality. Select quotes which will encourage students to develop varying descriptions of what kind of person this character might be. Write each quote on a separate slip of paper or index card.

For example, students preparing to read the novel *The BFG* by Roald Dahl will encounter a memorable Big Friendly Giant who has a penchant for hilariously mangled language. Character Quotes from his dialogue with the young girl Sophie provide students with an advance opportunity to explore his personality. (See *The BFG* example.)

Students in a history class studying the period of the development of the American West can be introduced to a Native American point of view through quotes taken from Chief Joseph's speech of surrender to government troops in 1877. (See Chief Joseph example.)

2 Next, organize students into cooperative groups of about three to four individuals. Give each group a different quote to consider. Each group then has the responsibility to generate as many words as they can that might describe this character based on their quote.

For example, different groups working on the BFG quotes might come up with: silly, sensitive, peace-loving, unintelligent, funny, lacks education, tries hard,

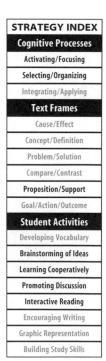

STRATEGY INDEX
Cognitive Processes
Activating/Focusing
Selecting/Organizing
Integrating/Applying
Text Frames
Cause/Effect
Concept/Definition
Problem/Solution
Compare/Contrast
Proposition/Support
Goal/Action/Outcome
Student Activities
Developing Vocabulary
Brainstorming of Ideas
Learning Cooperatively
Promoting Discussion
Interactive Reading
Encouraging Writing
Graphic Representation
Building Study Skills

Character Quotes from *The BFG* by Roald Dahl

- "I would so much love to have a jumbly big elefunt and go riding through green forests picking peachy fruits off the trees all day long."

- "I is never having a chance to go to school. I is full of mistakes. They is not my fault. I do my best."

- "Every human bean is diddly and different. Some is scrumdiddlyumptious and some is uckyslush."

- "If I come along and I is picking a lovely flower, if I is twisting the stem of the flower till it breaks, then the plant is screaming. I can hear it screaming and screaming very clear."

- "Human beans is squishing each other all the time. They is shootling guns and going up aerioplanes to drop their bombs on each other's head every week. Human beans is always killing other human beans."

- "I know exactly what words I am wanting to say, but somehow or other they is always getting squiff-squiddled around."

- "I is a dream-blowing giant. …I is scuddling away to other places to blow dreams into the bedrooms of sleeping children. Nice dreams. Lovely golden dreams. Dreams that is giving the dreamers a happy time."

— Dahl, R. (1982). *The BFG*. London, England: Puffin Books

Character Quotes from Chief Joseph

- "I want to have time to look for my children and see how many I can find. Maybe I shall find them among the dead."

- "I am tired; my heart is sick and sad. From where the sun now stands, I will fight no more forever."

- "You might as well expect the rivers to run backward as that any man who was born free should be contented penned up and denied liberty to go where he pleases…"

- "Good words will not give my people good health and stop them from dying. Good words will not get my people a home where they can live in peace and take care of themselves. I am tired of talk that comes to nothing."

- "We only ask an even chance to live as other men live. We ask to be recognized as men. We ask that the same law shall work alike on all men…"

- "All men were made by the same Great Spirit Chief. They are all brothers. The earth is the mother of all people, and all people shall have equal rights upon it."

- "Let me be a free man—free to travel, free to stop, free to work, free to trade where I choose, free to choose my own teachers, free to follow the religion of my fathers, free to think and talk and act for myself— and I will obey every law, or submit to the penalty."

crazy, looks at people as individuals, likes people, does nice things, lazy, a big guy, from another country, likes to dream, and so forth.

3 After each group has had sufficient time to generate their descriptors, ask a member from each group to (1) read their quote to the entire class, and (2) share their list of character qualities and traits that they associate with that character. At this time, inform the students that all their quotes were uttered by the same individual. Write these qualities and traits on the chalkboard or overhead transparency as they are presented by each group.

4 Involve the students in making some generalizations about this character or individual. Have the students work again in their cooperative groups to write a preliminary "personality profile" of this character, by using the qualities and traits listed by the entire class. The summary should contain four or five statements which integrate important qualities from the list.

5 The students are now ready to begin reading the story, novel, or other text assignment. After completing their reading, they can return to their "personality profiles" to discuss what new qualities or traits they might add and how they would change the profile to make it better match their understanding of the character. Students may also be asked to select further quotes that provide new information about their character, or they could identify representative quotes that lead to understanding a second character or individual. In addition, students could explore character qualities in their journal writing.

ADVANTAGES

Character Quotes can be used successfully in a number of settings and offer the following benefits:

• Students are introduced to several important facets of a character or individual's personality before they begin reading.

• Students are involved in actively predicting some of the major themes and issues of a story or selection.

• Students develop a fuller sense of the complexity of individuals through examination of a wide range of their words.

• This strategy is appropriate for any material than involves character study and is especially appropriate for literature and social studies contexts. The strategy may be adapted for use with students from elementary age through high school.

FURTHER RESOURCES

Blachowicz, C. (November, 1993). *Developing active comprehenders*. Paper presented at the meeting of the Madison Area Reading Council.

Concept Definition Mapping

"Look it up in the Dictionary!" Students are conditioned throughout their schooling to follow this advice. But for many students, using the dictionary results in associating very narrow and sometimes vague statements with the definition of a word. These dictionary statements usually contain little elaboration and may not connect at all to what students may already know about a word or concept.

Concept Definition Mapping (Schwartz and Raphael, 1985) is a strategy that helps enrich a student's understanding of a word or concept. Concept Definition Maps are graphic structures that focus students' attention on the key components of a definition: the class or category, properties or characteristics, and illustrations or examples. The strategy also encourages students to integrate their personal knowledge into a definition.

THE STRATEGY

Concept Definition Mapping is an excellent strategy for teaching key vocabulary and concepts. Using this strategy involves the following steps.

1 Display a blank Concept Definition Map on the overhead projector (see Concept Map example). Point out the questions that a complete definition would answer: What is it? What is it like? What are some examples of it?

2 Model how to use a concept definition map with your students by selecting a familiar concept and soliciting the relevant information for the map from the class. For example, students responding to a map for "cheese" might identify it as "food" or "a dairy product." Properties such as "is usually soft," "is usually yellow or white," "is made from milk," and "is kept cold" could be entered into the "What is it like?" boxes. And students might offer cheddar, Swiss, mozzarella, and limburger as examples.

3 Next, present a key new term or concept from the material the students are learning. Have the students work in pairs to create a word map for this new concept. Instruct the students to use information from the reading passage, the glossary or dictionary, and their own background knowledge to complete their word map.

Concept Definition Maps are graphic structures that focus students' attention on the key components of a definition.

For example, students studying different climatic regions of the earth might be given the concept "tundra" to map (see Science example). The textbook identifies a tundra as one of several characteristic geographical regions. Students would be able to note a number of properties of a tundra from the reading: the tundra has no trees; tundra vegetation consists mostly of grasses, mosses, and lichens; the tundra has temperatures below freezing most of the year; and the tundra has permanently frozen ground called permafrost. Some students may be able to add from their personal background knowledge that reindeer and caribou are found in tundra regions. Students would be able to locate examples of tundra from a world map in the textbook showing the different geographic regions. The tundra region is indicated in the Arctic areas of Alaska, Canada, Europe, and Russia.

4 When the students have finished constructing their word maps, have them use the maps to write a complete definition of the new concept. Emphasize that the definition should include the category of the word, some of its properties or characteristics, and specific examples. These definitions will be more involved than simple dictionary statements, and will usually contain several sentences.

A student definition for the concept "tundra" might be: *"The*

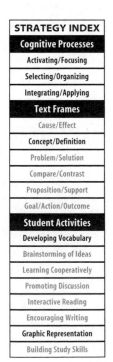

STRATEGY INDEX
Cognitive Processes
Activating/Focusing
Selecting/Organizing
Integrating/Applying
Text Frames
Cause/Effect
Concept/Definition
Problem/Solution
Compare/Contrast
Proposition/Support
Goal/Action/Outcome
Student Activities
Developing Vocabulary
Brainstorming of Ideas
Learning Cooperatively
Promoting Discussion
Interactive Reading
Encouraging Writing
Graphic Representation
Building Study Skills

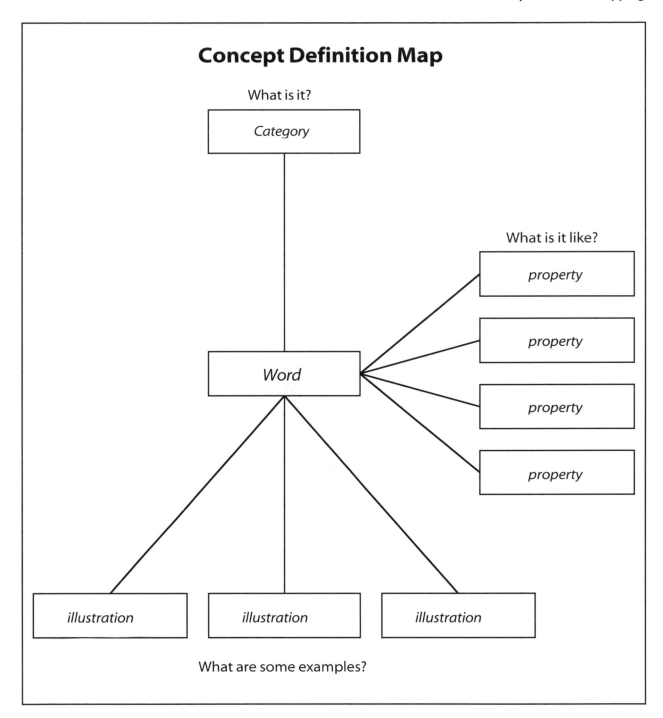

Concept Definition Map

What is it?

Category

What is it like?

property

property

property

property

Word

illustration   illustration   illustration

What are some examples?

Science Word Map - Tundra

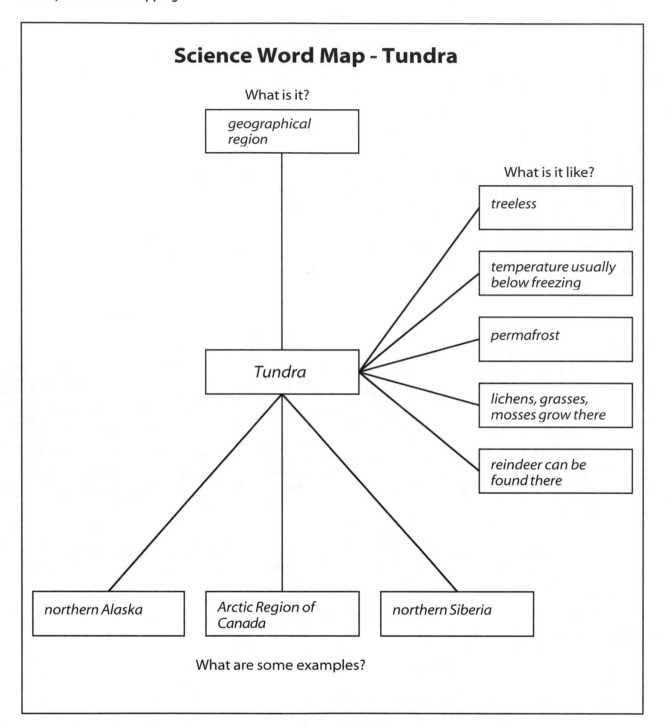

What is it?

geographical region

What is it like?

treeless

temperature usually below freezing

permafrost

lichens, grasses, mosses grow there

reindeer can be found there

Tundra

northern Alaska

Arctic Region of Canada

northern Siberia

What are some examples?

tundra is a region of the earth that has temperatures below freezing most of year. No trees grow there— only grasses, mosses, and lichens. The cold temperatures cause permafrost. The tundra is located in the far north, in Alaska, Canada, and Siberia."

5 Students can be assigned to create concept definition maps for other key terms and concepts from their reading. These maps can be used as review and study for tests.

ADVANTAGES

Concept Definition Maps offer a number of advantages:

- Students expand their understandings of key vocabulary and concepts beyond simple definitions.

- Students construct a visual representation of a concept's definition which helps them in remembering.

- Students are encouraged to integrate their personal background knowledge into a definition.

- This strategy may be used with students from elementary age through high school. Concept Definition Mapping can be successfully included in all content areas, and is especially effective with materials that have a heavy density of key vocabulary.

FURTHER RESOURCES

Santa, C. (1988). *Content reading including study systems.* Dubuque, IA: Kendall/Hunt.

Schwartz, R. & Raphael, T. (1985) Concept of definition: A key to improving students' vocabulary. *The Reading Teacher, 39,* 676-682.

Reading From Different Perspectives

Because students are who they are—individual people with different background experiences, beliefs, and understandings about the world—no two students will read and comprehend a passage in just the same way. A student whose grandfather

---

Reading from Different Perspectives guides students to consider ways of thinking other than their own.

---

is a dairy farmer will understand a passage about Holsteins in a decidedly different way than a student whose only connection to cows may be a *Far Side* cartoon. Likewise, a student who has been to Arizona will comprehend a story about the desert with a different appreciation than a student who has never left Wisconsin. Strategies which help students broaden their perspective about a topic will therefore help them read with a greater depth of comprehension and appreciation.

Reading from Different Perspectives (McNeil, 1984) is a teaching strategy that guides students through multiple readings of material in a way that makes them consider ways of thinking other than their own.

THE STRATEGY

The Reading from Different Perspectives strategy involves the following steps:

1 Have your students read through the story, article, or selection for the first time.

2 Identify a number of perspectives that could be connected to the important ideas or concepts of the passage. For example, some of the different perspectives on a history textbook passage about the building of transcontinental railroads might include *a Native American, a fur trapper, a homesteader,* and perhaps even *a buffalo.*

With fictional material, students may be assigned the perspective of characters in the story other than the narrator. Students reading the novel *To Kill a Mockingbird* by Harper Lee experience the story through the eyes of the young girl, Scout. Other perspectives from that book for students to consider could be her brother, Jem; the family cook, Calpurnia; the elderly neighbor, Mrs. Dubose; and the phantom neighbor, Boo Radley.

3 Divide the class into cooperative groups of three or four people and assign each group a different perspective.

4 To help students identify how someone with their assigned perspective would feel, have each group list (1) the ***concerns*** someone with their perspective might have about the topic, and (2) the ***needs*** a person of that perspective would have which could be affected by the topic. Use a *Different Perspective Graphic Outline* to provide structure for this activity (see railroad example).

For students working on different perspectives on the transcontinental railroad, ask: "What about the railroads would concern a Native American? A fur trapper? How would the railroads affect what buffalo would need? Homesteaders?" Have the students fill in the needs for their perspective and the concerns on the graphic outline. Students might decide that Native Americans would need their land, their food supply (the buffalo), and peace. Native Americans would be concerned about too many settlers arriving on the railroads, the loss of the buffalo, and increasing conflicts. Settlers would need supplies, markets for their products, and protection from the Indians. They would be concerned about railroad monopolies and high prices.

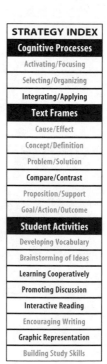

STRATEGY INDEX
Cognitive Processes
Activating/Focusing
Selecting/Organizing
Integrating/Applying
Text Frames
Cause/Effect
Concept/Definition
Problem/Solution
Compare/Contrast
Proposition/Support
Goal/Action/Outcome
Student Activities
Developing Vocabulary
Brainstorming of Ideas
Learning Cooperatively
Promoting Discussion
Interactive Reading
Encouraging Writing
Graphic Representation
Building Study Skills

Transcontinental Railroad Different Perspectives Graphic Outline

Your Perspective on   *The Railroads*

Role   *Buffalo*

Needs	**Concerns**
Grazing land	*Being killed*
Water	*Losing food*
Safety from predators	*Prairie not enough space to live in*
Lots of space to roam	

Read and React

Text Statements →	**Your Reactions**
— *RR got 20 sq.mi. for each mile of track.*	*"I won't have any space left to run."*
— *Buffalo Bill & hunters shot thousands of buffalo & left them to rot.*	*"This is murder! What kind of beasts are these humans?"*
— *Farmers followed the RR & plowed the prairie.*	*"There goes my food supply."*

Summary Position Statement

"The railroad destroyed our way of life on the prairies. It took up lots of land and brought people out who plowed up the grasses we eat. It also brought out hunters who murdered us by the thousands, not like the Indians who only killed a few of us for food. There are hardly any of us left!"

5 Next have the students re-read the material to look for specific statements or information that would be of special interest to their perspective. This information is written on the graphic outline, along with comments from the student's assigned perspective. For example, students re-reading from the point of view of a Buffalo would react to the statement "The railroad would obtain as much as 20 square miles of land for every mile of track" by noting that they would soon run out of grazing land. A passage describing the slaughter of the species by "Buffalo Bill Cody" and other hunters might elicit reactions about genocide from the students reading from the Buffalo perspective.

6 Discuss with students the insights they have gained through looking at the material from a variety of viewpoints. As a way of bringing their thoughts together, ask the students to write a position statement summarizing how someone of that perspective might feel. This statement is included on the bottom portion of the graphic outline.

ADVANTAGES

This strategy offers a number of advantages to the classroom teacher:

- Students are given a structure to re-read materials and to pick out ideas and information that they may have overlooked the first time through.

- Students develop empathy for points of view other than their own.

- Students are given practice in selecting specific information that relates to alternative ways of looking at a text.

- This strategy can be tailored to students from a range of grade levels, from elementary to high school. It can be applied in literature, social studies, science, and many other subject areas.

FURTHER RESOURCES

Cook, D. (Ed.). (1989). *Strategic learning in the content areas.* Madison, WI: Department of Public Instruction.

McNeil, J. (1984). *Reading comprehension: New directions for classroom practice.* Glenview, IL. Scott, Foresman, and Company.

Discussion Web

Teachers know that classroom discussions are an important way to encourage students to think. But involving the entire class in a discussion is a very difficult accomplishment. Too often, a few students are willing to contribute, and, as a result, they monopolize the conversation. What starts as a discussion ends up as a dialogue between the teacher and a handful of students. Meanwhile, the rest of the class sits passively by, with many students not bothering to listen in and pay attention to what is being said.

The Discussion Web (Alvermann, 1991) is a strategy that designs a class discussion so that all students actively participate. The Discussion Web incorporates all four language arts (reading, writing, speaking, and listening) and takes advantage of cooperative learning ideas to give students multiple opportunities to interact.

The Discussion Web incorporates all four language arts—reading, writing, speaking, and listening.

THE STRATEGY

The Discussion Web strategy involves the following steps:

1 Choose a selection for student reading that develops opposing viewpoints. An appropriate selection could be a story that elicits conflicting opinions of a character's actions or a section of a textbook which deals with controversial issues. Prepare students for reading by activating relevant background knowledge for the selection and setting their purposes for reading.

2 After students initially read the selection, introduce the Discussion Web and a focusing question for discussion (see "Industrial Revolution" example). Students reading a history textbook passage on the Industrial Revolution might be asked: "Did the Industrial Revolution help working people?" Students in a literature class reading *The Red Badge of Courage* by Stephen Crane might be asked after reading the early portions of the book, "Was Henry a coward for running?" Students reading the novel *Hatchet* by Gary Paulson might be asked, "Could Brian have survived in the wilderness without the hatchet?"

3 Assign students to work as partners to discuss the opposing sides of the question. As students work in pairs, they begin to flesh out the arguments on both sides of the Discussion Web, going back to the reading as needed. Students discussing *The Red Badge of Courage,* for example, may decide that the following events indicate cowardice: Henry ran at the beginning of the battle, he misled others about his running, and he felt shame for running. However, other factors argue against cowardice: he was experiencing his first battle, he had never been under fire before, and there was much confusion during the battle. This step establishes the evidence for both positions on the question.

4 When students have had sufficient time to share their viewpoints and jot them down on the Discussion Web, assign each pair of partners to work with another pair. This new group of four students is given the charge to work toward a consensus on the question. Additional arguments on both sides of the question are added to the Discussion Web. The group conclusion is written at the bottom of the web. For example, one group might conclude for *Hatchet* that although Brian could have gotten fire from other means and may have adapted to his plight by using different strategies, he probably would not have survived without the hatchet. A second group might argue that Brian's ingenuity and common sense toward using the hatchet could have

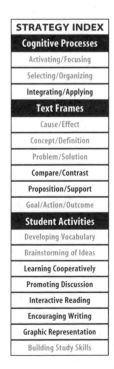

STRATEGY INDEX

Cognitive Processes
- Activating/Focusing
- Selecting/Organizing
- Integrating/Applying

Text Frames
- Cause/Effect
- Concept/Definition
- Problem/Solution
- Compare/Contrast
- Proposition/Support
- Goal/Action/Outcome

Student Activities
- Developing Vocabulary
- Brainstorming of Ideas
- Learning Cooperatively
- Promoting Discussion
- Interactive Reading
- Encouraging Writing
- Graphic Representation
- Building Study Skills

Discussion Web for The Industrial Revolution

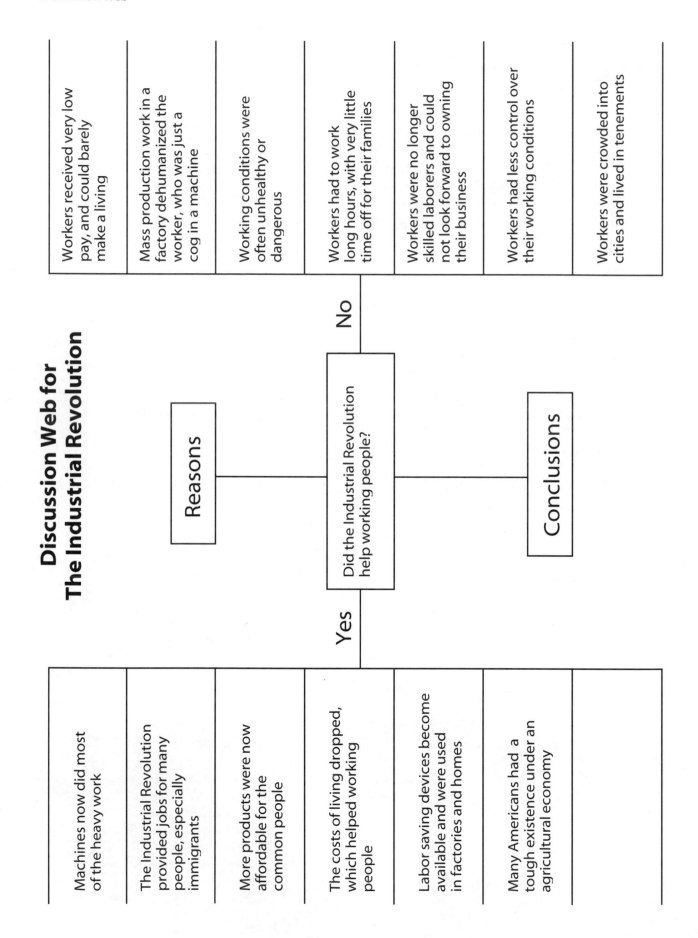

Reasons

Did the Industrial Revolution help working people?

Conclusions

No

- Workers received very low pay, and could barely make a living
- Mass production work in a factory dehumanized the worker, who was just a cog in a machine
- Working conditions were often unhealthy or dangerous
- Workers had to work long hours, with very little time off for their families
- Workers were no longer skilled laborers and could not look forward to owning their business
- Workers had less control over their working conditions
- Workers were crowded into cities and lived in tenements

Yes

- Machines now did most of the heavy work
- The Industrial Revolution provided jobs for many people, especially immigrants
- More products were now affordable for the common people
- The costs of living dropped, which helped working people
- Labor saving devices become available and were used in factories and homes
- Many Americans had a tough existence under an agricultural economy

been applied in other ways that would have helped him survive even without the hatchet.

5 Each group of four students is now ready to present its conclusions to the entire group. A spokesperson for each group is allowed approximately three minutes to discuss **one** reason for their conclusion. Allowing each group to present only one reason reduces the likelihood that the last groups to report will have no new ideas to offer. Spokespersons should also be encouraged to mention dissenting viewpoints from their group discussions.

6 Students are now prepared to write their own personal responses to the focusing question. The Discussion Web provides an organized guide to information and arguments that may be included in the writing. Students are thus able to develop their own ideas as well as reflect upon the contributions of their classmates as they write about the question.

ADVANTAGES

The Discussion Web strategy offers a number of advantages to classroom teachers:

- Students are active participants in the discussion throughout the entire process and they develop cooperative learning skills.

- Students are given a structure for evaluating both sides of an issue or question.

- Discussion Webs facilitate student writing which is well-organized and which develops support for positions.

- This strategy is especially useful for discussions in literature and the social studies.

- This strategy is appropriate for elementary age children up through high school age students.

FURTHER RESOURCES

Alvermann, D. (1991). The discussion web: A graphic aid for learning across the curriculum. *The Reading Teacher, 45*(2), 92-99.

Follow the Characters

"And the Oscar goes to..." The recent 1993 Academy Award nominations recognized movies that offered powerful messages to the viewers. *Schindler's List* told the story of a mercenary opportunist who came to risk everything to save the lives of his workers during the Holocaust. *The Piano* focused on the metamorphosis of an isolated young mute woman into a person able to enter into a trusting relationship and reenter the world. *In the Name of the Father* followed the evolution of a petty criminal into a man who came to understand himself and his father. And *The Remains of the Day* painfully chronicled the inability of a staid English butler to acknowledge his emotions and break out of his heavily patterned existence. In different ways, each of these movies communicated important ideas through how the characters experienced change in the face of various conflicts.

Change and conflict are two of the constants of life that underlie fictional literature. By examining how characters handle the story's conflict and how they change, students can develop insight into the author's point of view. Follow the Characters (Buehl, 1994) is a strategy that helps students understand stories

---

By examining how characters handle the story's conflict and how they change, students can develop insight into the author's point of view.

---

through character analysis. Follow the Characters involves organizing key information about a character into a grid. The resulting visual outline helps students decide upon the author's theme or message in a story.

THE STRATEGY

Follow the Characters is a strategy that works both for short stories and longer works of fictional literature. Using the strategy with students involves the following steps:

1 Review the basic components of story structure (see the Story Mapping strategy on page 103). Establish that stories have a setting, characters, plot events, conflict and its resolution, and author's theme.

2 Next, use the role of a "detective" as a metaphor for helping students conceptualize the process of character analysis. Ask students how a detective goes about solving a mystery. They will likely answer that a detective looks for clues and investigates people. Emphasize that this detective frame of mind will also help them discover the author's theme of the story. For clues about the author's point in the story, they should "follow the characters." (See Follow the Characters graphic.) Following the characters means that a reader "tunes in" to what a character does or says and what others do or say about this character. Readers should pay special attention to the role of the character in the story's conflict and whether this role changes the character in any way.

3 Place a blank character analysis grid (see *Duel* example) on the overhead projector and model with students using a familiar story. Select a well-known story such as a fairy tale or a short story that the students have previously read. Fill in the major character in the center circle and identify the nature of the conflict (or conflicts) in the story: within a person, between people, or between people and nature. The conflict is recorded in the ring around the character circle.

For example, most younger students have encountered the story of Aladdin, perhaps through the recent animated movie. Most students would recognize that the major conflict in this fairy tale is between Aladdin and the evil Jafar. Some may also realize that Aladdin has an inner conflict when it comes to being truthful.

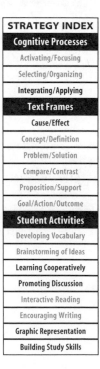

STRATEGY INDEX

Cognitive Processes
Activating/Focusing
Selecting/Organizing
Integrating/Applying

Text Frames
Cause/Effect
Concept/Definition
Problem/Solution
Compare/Contrast
Proposition/Support
Goal/Action/Outcome

Student Activities
Developing Vocabulary
Brainstorming of Ideas
Learning Cooperatively
Promoting Discussion
Interactive Reading
Encouraging Writing
Graphic Representation
Building Study Skills

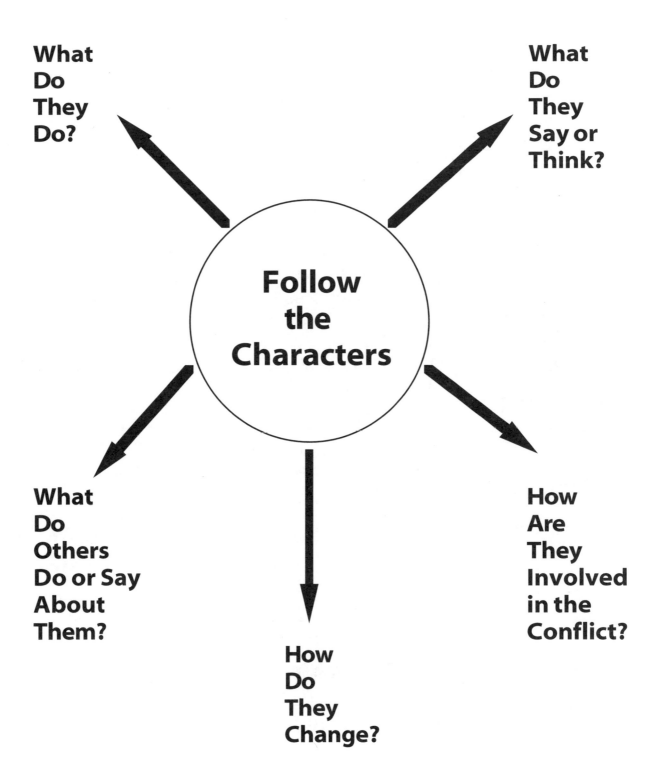

What
Do
They
Do?

What
Do
They
Say or
Think?

**Follow
the
Characters**

What
Do
Others
Do or Say
About
Them?

How
Do
They
Change?

How
Are
They
Involved
in the
Conflict?

"Duel" Character Analysis Grid

1. What does the character do?

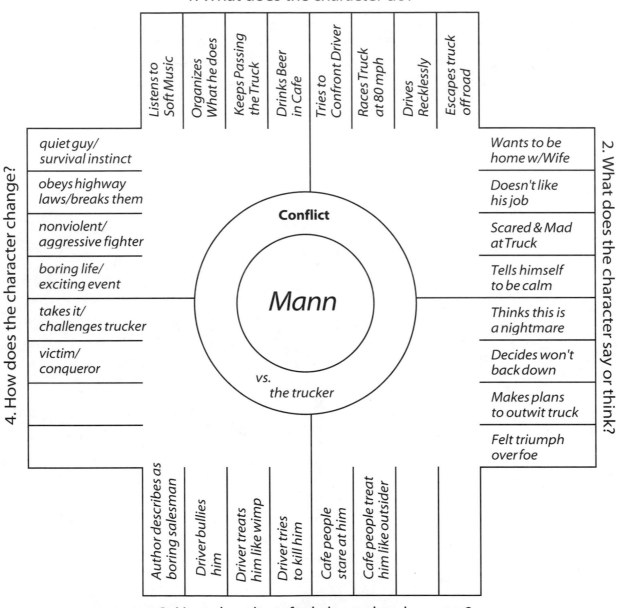

1. What does the character do?

Listens to Soft Music | Organizes What he does | Keeps Passing the Truck | Drinks Beer in Cafe | Tries to Confront Driver | Races Truck at 80 mph | Drives Recklessly | Escapes truck off road

4. How does the character change?

quiet guy/ survival instinct
obeys highway laws/breaks them
nonviolent/ aggressive fighter
boring life/ exciting event
takes it/ challenges trucker
victim/ conqueror

Conflict

Mann

vs. the trucker

2. What does the character say or think?

Wants to be home w/Wife
Doesn't like his job
Scared & Mad at Truck
Tells himself to be calm
Thinks this is a nightmare
Decides won't back down
Makes plans to outwit truck
Felt triumph over foe

Author describes as boring salesman | Driver bullies him | Driver treats him like wimp | Driver tries to kill him | Cafe people stare at him | Cafe people treat him like outsider

3. How do others feel about the character?

5. Author's Theme or Point of View:

4 Next elicit from the students information about this character that would fit in the first three quadrants of the grid: *what does the character do, what does the character say or think*, and *how do others feel about the character*. Note that "others" might also include how the author or narrator feels about the character, in addition to the other characters in the story. Then, using the information recorded in these three quadrants, help the students formulate the changes experienced by this character, to be listed as before/after comparisons, in the last quadrant. Finally, help the students articulate possible ways of stating the author's theme or point of view, given the character changes you have identified.

In our *Aladdin* exmple students might note that he steals things, he does daring acts, and he fights to save the princess.They may recall that he lies to the princess, regrets his lie, and tells the genie what he wants for his life. They may also observe that others regard him as a thief, a poor person, a liar, a victim, and a hero. He changes during the story to value honesty and put someone else's well-being ahead of his own. Finally, students might articulate the theme of *Aladdin* as "A person should be true to himself," or "Bad behavior will eventually be a person's downfall."

5 The students are now ready to apply the character analysis grid to a new story. After they have completed reading the story, have them work with partners to complete the conflict ring and first three quadrants. Then team the partners with a second set of partners to work on the character changes in the fourth quadrant. Based on their analysis, have each group write their version of the author's theme. Students would complete additional character analysis grids for stories that feature more than one major character.

For example, students reading the short story *Duel* by Richard Matheson would analyze the major character, Mann, who is menaced by an unknown trucker on a deserted highway. (See *Duel* example.) As students examine Mann's actions and thoughts, they find that the conflict changes Mann from a quiet, rather nondescript individual to someone involved in a dangerous competition on the highway. Students might express the author's theme as "You can only push a person so far before they have to fight back," or "We all have a survival instinct inside us to make us want to defend ourselves."

ADVANTAGES

Follow the Characters is a strategy that can enhance student understanding of literature in a number of ways:

- Students are provided with a systematic way to attack a story to get at its meaning.

- Students learn to recognize the central roles of conflict and change in character development.

- Students develop a visual outline of major elements of a story, upon which they can rely as they grapple with articulating the author's theme or point of view.

- This strategy is appropriate for most narrative literature. It can be modified for use with students at all levels, from elementary age through high school.

FURTHER RESOURCES

Beck, I., & McKeown, M. (November/December 1981). Developing questions that promote comprehension: The story map. *Language Arts*, 913-918.

Buehl, D. (May, 1994). Persona: Character analysis sheds light on story's meaning. *WEAC News & Views*, 21.

Frayer Model

What makes a vegetable a vegetable? What do all vegetables have in common? How are vegetables different from fruits? Can certain edible weeds be counted as vegetables? How about mushrooms? Is wheat a vegetable?

Developing concepts with students involves far more than teaching definitions. The Frayer Model (Frayer, Frederick, and Klausmeier, 1969) provides an excellent format for deepening student understandings of important concepts. Using this model

---

Developing concepts with students involves far more than teaching definitions.

---

with students will help them differentiate between characteristics which define the concept, and those which may merely be associated with it. The Frayer Model also provides a visual way of distinguishing between items which represent the concept and items which are lacking some key characteristic of the concept.

THE STRATEGY

The Frayer Model is a graphic organizer which contains four compartments for recording the information related to a concept (see "vegetable" example). A Frayer Model grid could be given to students as a worksheet or could be developed by the teacher on the chalkboard or overhead transparency. It could also become a study guide for students as they read.

Using the Frayer Model involves the following steps:

1 Carefully analyze the concept you will be teaching to your students. Create a list of all necessary characteristics or attributes that any example of this concept must hold. For example, if you were teaching the concept "reptile," your essential characteristics would include animal, cold-blooded, and vertebrate. Essential characteristics for the concept

"vegetable" would include nutritious food found in non-woody plants and contains vitamins and/or minerals.

2 Introduce the concept to the students and have them generate examples of it. One method could be to break students into cooperative groups with the task of listing as many examples of the concept as they can. For "reptile" students may list snakes, alligators, lizards, and crocodiles. Questions are likely to emerge at this point. Are frogs reptiles? Salamanders? Fish?

3 On the board or overhead transparency, solicit these examples from your students. Encourage them to add to the list or to challenge examples already offered. Start a second list with your students detailing what these examples all seem to have in common. During this phase, students began to identify the key characteristics of a concept.

4 The students are now ready to read a selection about the concept. Distribute blank Frayer Model grids to be used as an exercise while reading. Highlight the information that needs to be entered in each section: *essential characteristics* (what all have), *nonessential characteristics* (what some have and others don't), *examples* (these are…"reptiles"), and *nonexamples* (these are not…"reptiles"). Note that students will be reading to confirm or reject the information generated from the class. You may wish to have students work in pairs as they read and complete the grid.

5 When the students have completed their reading, go back to your original list generated by students on this concept. On a Frayer Model grid on the board or overhead transparency, place those examples and characteristics that students were able to confirm by the reading. Other characteristics and examples may

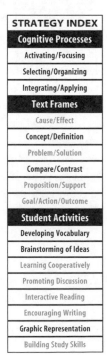

STRATEGY INDEX

Cognitive Processes
Activating/Focusing
Selecting/Organizing
Integrating/Applying

Text Frames
Cause/Effect
Concept/Definition
Problem/Solution
Compare/Contrast
Proposition/Support
Goal/Action/Outcome

Student Activities
Developing Vocabulary
Brainstorming of Ideas
Learning Cooperatively
Promoting Discussion
Interactive Reading
Encouraging Writing
Graphic Representation
Building Study Skills

Frayer Model

Essential Characteristics	Nonessential Characteristics

is a nutritious food
contains vitamins & minerals
comes from non-woody plants
is a direct part of a plant:
  stem,
  leaf,
  bulb,
  root,
  tuber,
  seed, or
  fruit
	color
	which part of plant is eaten
	whether grows above ground
	  or below ground
	whether eaten raw or cooked
	size
	planted from seeds

Examples
 	
beans
carrots
cucumber   herbs?
potatoes   watermelon?
squash   strawberries?
radish
lettuce
rutabaga
kohlrabi
peas
asparagus
	Nonexamples
	
	tree fruit, such as
	  apples,
	  cherries,
	  oranges
	
	mushrooms
	
	sugar, honey, maple syrup
	
	woody vine plants,
	  such as grapes
	
	woody cane plants,
	  such as raspberries

Vegetable

then be placed in the nonessential and nonexamples sections. Students should also be encouraged to offer the new information they learned from the reading to the appropriate section on the grid. Further study may be needed to place some examples. We call watermelons and strawberries fruit, but don't they fit the definition of vegetable? Do herbs have nutritional value? Can wheat be eaten as a vegetable, like corn, or does it need to be processed first?

6 When completed, the Frayer Model grid provides students with organized information that can easily be used for written assignments and for studying for a test.

ADVANTAGES

The Frayer Model strategy offers a number of advantages to the classroom teacher:

- Students are provided with a visual structure to help them develop a more sophisticated understanding of an important concept.

- Students are guided into differentiating between characteristics which define the concept and those which may be sometimes associated with it.

- Students are able to distinguish between examples of the concept and other items which share only some of the defining characteristics.

- The Frayer Model can be used as a strategy for lessons in all subject areas. It works especially well in teaching science concepts.

FURTHER RESOURCES

Frayer, D., Frederick, W., & Klausmeier, H. (1969) A schema for testing the level of cognitive mastery. *Working Paper No. 16.* Madison, WI: Wisconsin Research and Development Center.

Cook, D., (Ed.). (1989). *Strategic learning in the content areas.* Madison, WI: Department of Pubic Instruction.

© 1995 Wisconsin State Reading Association, Doug Buehl, *Classroom Strategies for Interactive Learning*

Guided Imagery

You are in the dark, forbidding forests of 18th Century North America. There is danger in the air as you march along. You remain in formation, even though you sense that an ambush is forming all around you. You hear nothing but the tramping feet of your fellow soldiers. Yet as you glance about you think you see a glimpse of movement through the dense underbrush. Suddenly a war cry rips through the air from the thick foliage to the left of you. The Hurons!

The scene described above was based upon an episode from the recent motion picture *Last of the Mohicans*. Sitting in the theater, it was almost impossible for moviegoers not to feel that they were personally experiencing the French and Indian War—the tension, fear, and excitement of an impending conflict.

Guided Imagery is a strategy that helps trigger visualization for students as they read and learn.

Our imaginations placed us onto the screen, next to the characters of the story, and helped us identify with their lives and the historical events portrayed in the film.

As teachers, we know that showing a movie can help students "get a feeling" for what they read. But effective readers are also able to generate these images for themselves as they read. Guided Imagery (Bagley, 1987) is a strategy that helps trigger visualization for students as they read and learn. For many students, textbooks are an endless parade of terms and facts. Helping students visualize what they are reading brings the material to life and makes it more meaningful.

THE STRATEGY

Guided Imagery is a strategy that capitalizes on children's active imaginations. Activities such as role playing, pretending, and daydreaming are natural elements of children's play. Guided Imagery in the classroom involves the following steps.

1 To "warm up" students to using imagery, tell them you are going to suggest some things that they are going to see in their minds. Have each student work with a partner. As you suggest an image, have the students describe to their partners what they are seeing with their "mind's eye." You might suggest images such as a storm, a building, an animal, a food, a relative, or a sporting event. Allow the students a few moments to elaborate upon the image they are forming in their minds before sharing it with their partner.

2 Next, have the students preview the selection they will be reading. Emphasize that they should give special attention to any pictures, drawings, or graphics that are included with the text. This is especially important for text materials in science or social studies which typically feature a number of visuals to enhance the information. As students attend to these visual elements of the text, they begin to "see" what the material is about. You may also wish to use other sources for pictures that will stimulate the students' imaginations.

3 Guided Imagery can be used either to prepare students for a reading or to deepen their understanding after they have read. Because most students could readily visualize many of the hardships experienced by the pioneers traveling west across the Great Plains, Guided Imagery could help introduce the textbook passage. However, students would probably need to read the passage on photosynthesis first to acquire some basic knowledge before they could successfully visualize what it would be like to be inside a plant as it went through this process.

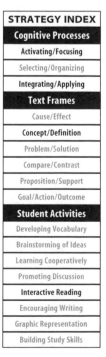

STRATEGY INDEX
Cognitive Processes
Activating/Focusing
Selecting/Organizing
Integrating/Applying
Text Frames
Cause/Effect
Concept/Definition
Problem/Solution
Compare/Contrast
Proposition/Support
Goal/Action/Outcome
Student Activities
Developing Vocabulary
Brainstorming of Ideas
Learning Cooperatively
Promoting Discussion
Interactive Reading
Encouraging Writing
Graphic Representation
Building Study Skills

Guided Imagery

(Social Studies Example)

"The Great Plains"

Imagine that you are in Nebraska. It is Summer, 1887 and you are standing in the midst of rolling prairie for as far as you can see in all directions.

Look around and see that no trees, no buildings, and no other human beings are anywhere in sight.

Notice the wind gently swaying the two-foot tall prairie grasses back and forth.

Feel the 90 degree heat from the hot noon sun as it beats down upon you.

Breathe in the dust and pollen from the grasses around you and imagine wiping the grimy sweat from your forehead.

Notice the tired ox standing next to your single-bladed steel plow.

See yourself trudging over to the plow and placing your hands on its rough wooden handles.

Watch the hard-packed deep black prairie soil turn over from your plow blade as you struggle along behind the ox.

Feel the blisters on your hands as they grip the plow handles.

Imagine the strain on your back muscles, and on your arms and legs as the plow jerks you along.

Labor your way over a small hill, and in the distance notice the small hut made with thick squares of prairie sod.

Leave the plow and slowly make your way closer to the hut, noticing it in greater and greater detail.

Bend your head as you enter the dark, dank sod hut and slowly pace around on its cement hard dirt floor.

4 Tell the students to close their eyes, take several deep breaths, and relax as much as they can. Introduce the exercise by giving them some background for the situation they will be visualizing. Encourage them to make use of all of their senses as they imagine—sight, sound, physical sensations, and emotions. Suggest the image to the students one sentence at a time, and pause for several seconds after each sentence to allow them time to process what you are saying and to visualize the picture.

For example, to prepare students for a reading about the rigors of farming in the Great Plains during the 1880's, you might say: "You are going to imagine what it was like to be a homesteader on the Great Plains in the late nineteenth century. You will be alone and you will be seeing the prairie much the way it was before the settlers came." (See Social Studies Guided Imagery example.)

To prepare students for a Guided Imagery exercise on photosynthesis, you might say, "Think about some of the things you would find in a factory, some of the machines, the workers, the raw materials, the energy source, and so on. Now imagine that you can shrink to a size so tiny that you can walk right through the pore of a leaf. You are now in a photosynthesis factory." And you could continue with suggestions that would help the students visualize the process of photosynthesis in this plant. (For an excellent example of a photosynthesis Guided Imagery, see Lazear, 1991.)

5 Ask the students to share their reflections about what they were imagining during the exercise. What did they notice with their imaginations? Do they have any questions about what they were attempting to visualize? This would also be an excellent opportunity to have students write about what they visualized, as a way of summarizing their insights about the situation.

6 As students gain practice in visualizing, they can be asked to create their own Guided Imagery exercises in cooperative groups. Students may also work with partners, taking turns describing what they visualized as they read parts of the text.

ADVANTAGES

Guided Imagery is an strategy that supports learning in a number of ways:

- Students are stimulated to generate their own images when they read.

- Creating vivid mental images of ideas and concepts helps students remember information longer.

- Students who are more visual learners become actively involved with their reading. This is especially true for many low achieving students.

- Students find imagery techniques motivational, and they become more personally engaged with the material.

- This strategy is appropriate for students from elementary age to high school. Guided Imagery is a strategy that can be effectively used with materials in all content areas, from introducing the setting for a short story to deepening the understanding of science concepts.

FURTHER RESOURCES

Bagley, M. (1987) *Imagery to develop memory.* Monroe, NY: Trillium Press.

Lazear, D. (1991). *Seven ways of teaching: The artistry of teaching with multiple intelligences.* Palatine, IL: Skylight Publishing.

History Change Frame

What's the point of all this? For many students, history seems like a never ending series of facts: names, dates, places, events. Students can begin to make more sense of history if they are able to use those facts to help them understand the important *changes* people have experienced. Changes tend to create problems that people have to confront. Learning about these changes helps us better understand who we are and what we have to deal with today.

Teaching students to read history textbooks from a problem/solution frame of mind enables them to cue

---

Students can begin to make more sense of history if they are able to understand the important changes people have experienced.

---

into the major changes that are being discussed in a chapter. The Change Frame (Buehl, 1992) is a strategy that helps students avoid getting bogged down in the details of what they are reading. Instead, the Change Frame focuses student attention on groups of people who are trying to solve problems brought about by change.

THE STRATEGY

The Change Frame strategy is an excellent strategy to use with students when introducing the history textbook or readings. The strategy involves the following steps:

1 Select several time periods that will be covered in the class. In a brainstorming exercise, ask students **who** they expect will be featured in a reading for each time period. Emphasize that they should think of *groups* of people, not individual people. "What groups of people would you expect to read about during American Revolution?" "The Settling of the American West?" "The Vietnam War?" Student answers for each

time period could be angry colonists and the British; pioneers, cowboys, and Indians; and antiwar protesters, the U.S. Army, and communist guerrillas.

2 Introduce the Change Frame on an overhead transparency (see Change Frame graphic). In your discussion note that history tends to focus on people who must try to solve problems which are caused by change. Factual details in a chapter are presented to help the reader understand the problems and people's actions to solve these problems.

3 Direct students into the chapter to be assigned for reading. Have them survey the chapter to determine what groups will be the focus of the material. You may need to model this process by thinking aloud as you examine the title, headings and subheadings, chapter objectives, advance organizers, primary source excerpts, pictures, and graphics. Determine with students **who** "the players" are in this chapter. Who is featured?

4 Next ask students to continue to survey the chapter to look for clues about problems these groups of people might be encountering. "What problems would the pioneers face in the old West? The Indians?" "What problems concerned women in the Progressive Age? Black Americans? Muckrakers?" In some cases, the people in the chapter may be actually causing problems that others must deal with. "What problems came about because of the Robber Barons in the 1870's and 80's?"

5 Assign a portion of the chapter to be read. As students read, they fill out the Change Frame Graphic Organizer (see example for the American West), selecting information which identifies the changes which are causing the problems for each group of

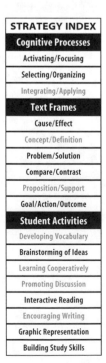

STRATEGY INDEX

Cognitive Processes
Activating/Focusing
Selecting/Organizing
Integrating/Applying

Text Frames
Cause/Effect
Concept/Definition
Problem/Solution
Compare/Contrast
Proposition/Support
Goal/Action/Outcome

Student Activities
Developing Vocabulary
Brainstorming of Ideas
Learning Cooperatively
Promoting Discussion
Interactive Reading
Encouraging Writing
Graphic Representation
Building Study Skills

© 1995 Wisconsin State Reading Association, Doug Buehl, *Classroom Strategies for Interactive Learning*

Change Frame

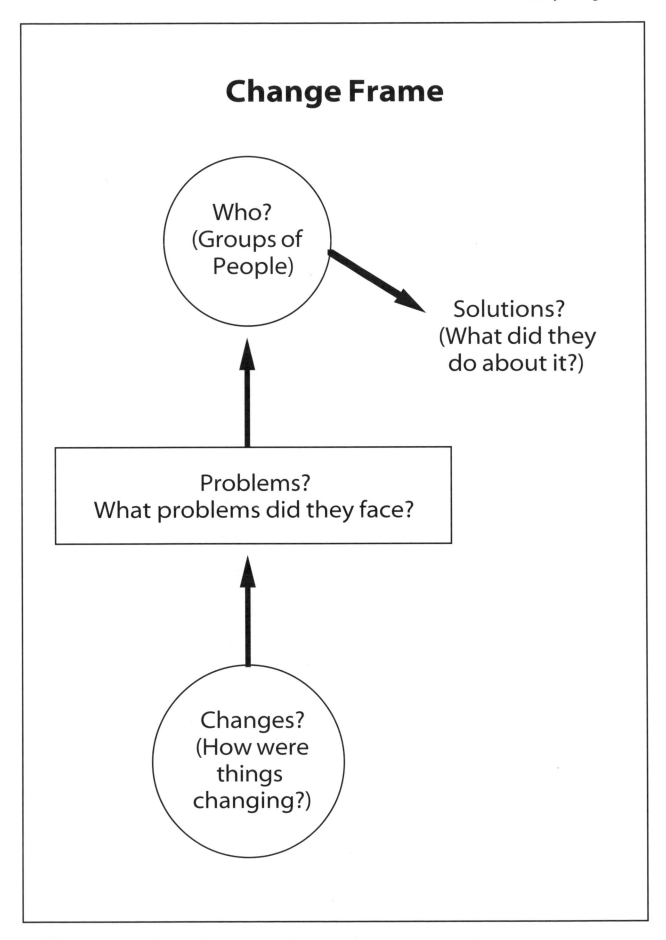

© 1995 Wisconsin State Reading Association, Doug Buehl, *Classroom Strategies for Interactive Learning*   57

Change Frame Graphic Organizer

Who? _Indians_	Who? _Cattle Ranchers_	Who? _Prairie Farmers_
What problems did they face? • Less land to live on • Disappearance of Buffalo • Conflicts with settlers • Many were killed	What problems did they face? • End of the Open Range • Conflicts with Indians • Conflicts with farmers and sheep ranchers	What problems did they face? • Conflicts with Indians • Conflicts with cattle ranchers • Hard life on the prairie
What changes caused these problems? • Increased numbers of settlers coming West • Discovery of gold and other metals • Homestead Act • The Railroad	What changes caused these problems? • More settlers who wanted to farm and fence off the prairie • Homestead Act • The Railroad	What changes caused these problems? • Homestead Act • Harsh weather • The Railroad
What did they do to solve the problems? • Fought the settlers and soldiers • Agreed to treaties • Left reservations • Changed their way of life	What did they do to solve the problems? • Got help from Army against Indians • Range wars • Accepted fenced prairie	What did they do to solve the problems? • Got help from Army against Indians • Fenced in the prairie • Adapted to harsh conditions: dry farming, new machines

people. They also identify actions taken by each group to solve their problems.

For example, changes which affected Indians in the Old West included a huge increase in white settlers (a demographic change), the discovery of gold and other minerals (an economic change), and the Homestead Act (a legal change).

6 Discuss with students how changes have affected people in different ways. For example, both the building of the transcontinental railroad and

---

Students come to see that the information included in a history chapter is not a series of randomly selected facts.

---

the passing of the Homestead Act affected all three groups of people in the American West. "How did the railroad cause different problems for the Indians, the cattle ranchers, and the prairie farmers?" "How about the Homestead Act?"

Students come to realize that the impact of changes varies depending on which group of people is considered. Sometimes a change benefits one group and causes problems for others. These differences are clearly portrayed on a Change Frame Graphic Organizer.

ADVANTAGES

The Change Frame strategy offers a number of advantages to the classroom teacher of history:

- Students are given a structure to sort through a wealth of material so that they get the point of the chapter.

- Students come to see that the information included in a history chapter is not a series of randomly selected facts.

- Students see how the information fits together, and have a construct of making sense of what they read. The problem/solution frame enables students to see patterns in history and helps them develop a coherent understanding of what history is and why we study it.

- The Change Frame Graphic Organizer provides an excellent blueprint for writing assignments and other follow-up activities. Relevant information is clearly organized to allow relationships to be established and comparisons to be made.

- This strategy is appropriate for elementary age children up through high school age students.

FURTHER RESOURCES

Buehl, D. (1992). A frame of mind for reading history. *The Exchange.* Secondary Reading Interest Group Newsletter, 5(1).

KWL-Plus—
Know/Want to Know/Learned

A persistent challenge for teachers is to encourage students to be active thinkers while they read. Active readers make predictions about what they will be reading. Before they start, active readers consider what they already know about the story or topic. Then as they read, they confirm whether or not their predictions were on target. Active readers have an idea of what to look for, and when they are done, they evaluate what they have learned or experienced.

Students make predictions about what they will be reading through the generation of questions they would like answered.

Many of our students are not active readers, and they are confused about what they should be thinking as they read. The KWL-Plus strategy (Carr and Ogle, 1987) is a technique that helps students take stock of what they know before they dive into a reading assignment. Using this strategy with students will help them make predictions about what they will be reading through the generation of questions they would like to have answered. The strategy also helps students to organize what they have learned when they are finished reading.

THE STRATEGY

KWL is an acronym which stands for *Know, Want to Know, and Learned*. The strategy involves using a three column graphic organizer with students (see example). The graphic organizer becomes the students' study guide as they read. The graphic organizer could be given to students as a worksheet or could be developed by the teacher on the chalkboard or overhead transparency.

Using the KWL-Plus strategy involves the following steps:

1 List the main topic of the story or selection on the top of the KWL grid. Ask students to contribute what they know, or think they know, about the topic. These contributions are recorded in the first column (*K—What We Know*). For example, students preparing to read a story about Eskimos might contribute: "live in the far north," "ice and snow," "igloos," "warm clothes made from sealskins," "sled dogs," and other such items. A selection involving rattlesnakes might elicit: "poisonous," "fangs," "diamondbacks," "live in deserts," "shake rattles as warning."

2 As this information is shared, questions are likely to emerge. "Are all rattlesnakes poisonous?" "Will you die if you get bit?" "Do they always rattle before they strike?" These are natural questions that students might have about rattlesnakes, and they should be recorded in the middle column (*W—What We Want to Learn*). Ask the students whether there are other questions they would like answered about rattlesnakes. For instance, "Do they live in Wisconsin?" "What do they look like?"

3 Guide the students in categorizing their knowledge and questions. This is recorded in a list entitled "Categories of Information We Expect to Use." Categories for rattlesnakes might include: where they live (location), what they do (abilities), how they look (description), and their effects on people (people).

4 The students are now ready to read the story or selection. Encourage them to look for information that answers their questions or expands their understanding of the topic.

5 When the students have completed their reading, focus attention on the third column of the grid (*L—What We Have Learned*). Ask students to offer the new information that

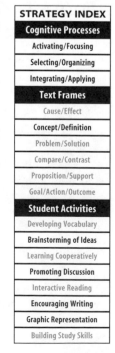

STRATEGY INDEX

Cognitive Processes
Activating/Focusing
Selecting/Organizing
Integrating/Applying

Text Frames
Cause/Effect
Concept/Definition
Problem/Solution
Compare/Contrast
Proposition/Support
Goal/Action/Outcome

Student Activities
Developing Vocabulary
Brainstorming of Ideas
Learning Cooperatively
Promoting Discussion
Interactive Reading
Encouraging Writing
Graphic Representation
Building Study Skills

KWL Grid for a Reading on Rattlesnakes:

Topic: Rattlesnakes

K (Know)	W (Want to Know)	L (Learned)
• They have sharp fangs	• What do they look like?	A—all are poisonous
• They are poisonous	• Are all rattlesnakes poisonous?	A—often warn before bite
• They live in deserts	• Will you die if you get bit by a rattlesnake?	D—member of pit viper family
• They shake their rattles before striking	• Do all rattlesnakes rattle before biting?	L—28 varieties found from Canada to S. America
• Diamondbacks are a type	• Do any live in Wisconsin?	L—most found in deserts
• They live in holes	• What medicine stops the poison?	L—some found in Midwest
• They eat mice		D—rattle is set of horny pieces joined together
		P—bite can be fatal to small children
		P—some bites can kill adults
		A—young born live rather than from eggs

Categories of Information We Expect to Use:

1. Where they live (L—Location)

2. What they do (A—Abilities)

3. How they look (D—Description)

4. How they affect people (P—People)

© 1995 Wisconsin State Reading Association, Doug Buehl, *Classroom Strategies for Interactive Learning*

Rattlesnake Concept Map

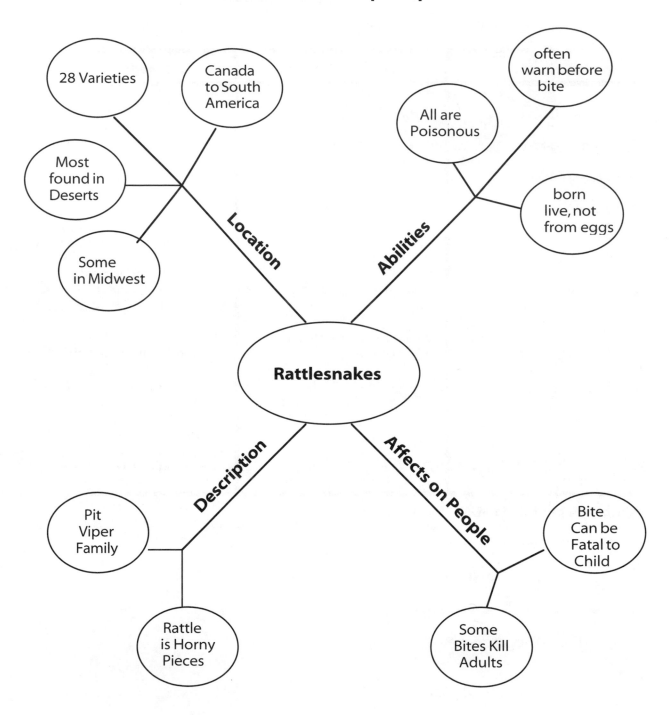

they discovered in the reading and record this on the grid. Ask what category this new information fits under (for our rattle-snake example: *location, abilities, description,* or *people*) and indicate the appropriate code. New categories may also emerge. Experienced students may be able to complete this step independently, by filling out the new information on a KWL worksheet, but many students will need guidance and direction from the teacher in organizing this information.

6 When the KWL grid in completed, a concept map which brings together all the information under each category can be created, either on the chalkboard or by individual students. (See Rattlesnake Concept Map example.) In this way, the information is organized for student writing assignments or other projects. Questions from the middle column (*Want to Know*) that are not answered by the reading provide the basis for independent projects and research.

ADVANTAGES

The KWL Plus strategy offers a number of advantages to the classroom teacher:

- KWL provides teachers with an inventory of student background knowledge about a topic.

- Students are given a structure for making predictions about what they will be reading.

- Students develop self-questioning skills and learn to read actively to answer their questions about a topic.

- Students are guided into meaningful organization of new information.

- KWL Plus can be used as a strategy for lessons in social studies, science, math, and other subject areas.

FURTHER RESOURCES

Carr, E.G., & Ogle D. (1987). KWL Plus: A strategy for comprehension and summarization. *Journal of Reading, 30*(7), 626-631.

Cook, D. (Ed.). (1989). *Strategic learning in the content areas.* Madison, WI: Department of Public Instruction.

LINK—
List/Inquire/Note/Know

Suppose as you paged through a magazine, you happened upon an article entitled "Lasers: The Promise of a Space-Age Technology." What would you anticipate about this article? Laser weapons? Laser surgery? Computer printers and other laser tools? Laser discs? Spectacular light shows? The principles behind lasers as a beam of

---

Students are involved in directing their own discussion about what they know about a topic.

---

light? Like any mature reader, you would anticipate the content of what you would be reading by reaching into your memory and marshaling pertinent information that might connect to new material in the article. Effective readers take stock of what they know before they start.

LINK (Vaughan and Estes, 1986) is a brainstorming strategy that prompts students to anticipate what they will encounter in a reading. An additional feature of the strategy is that students are involved in directing their own discussion about what they know about a topic.

THE STRATEGY

LINK is an acronym for List, Inquire, Note, and Know. The strategy involves the following steps.

1 Determine a key word or concept related to the material that will trigger responses from your students. Write this "cue" word on the chalkboard or on an overhead transparency. Allow about three minutes for the students to *list* on a piece of paper the associations they have for this "cue" word. For example, the cue words "solar system" might be appropriate for a sixth grade class preparing to read a science selection related to this topic.

2 Solicit associations from the students and write them around the cue word on the transparency.

Limit responses to one per student. It may be desirable to start with less active students to increase their involvement and to insure that all students will be able to contribute. When everyone has offered an association, allow for students to respond with further ideas. During this stage, student contributions are listed *without comment* from either the teacher or the students, including the individuals responding. Sixth graders, for example, would probably be able to offer a rich assortment of associations for the cue words "solar system" (see Solar System LINK example).

3 Encourage students to *inquire* about the items listed on the transparency. The students may ask for clarification or elaboration of some of the items, or they may ask for examples or a definition. Students may even challenge some of the items. Inquiries are directed to their fellow students, not the teacher.

During the inquiry step, students interact both to share and to extend their understandings of the cue word or concept. To help students take on this responsibility, some classroom ground rules might help. For example, students may need to be reminded to be respectful of each other during their inquiries, taking care not to embarrass or belittle their classmates as they examine the items. In our example, students might question associations such as *solar cells* or *solarium*. The resulting discussion could establish the connection between the solar system (the sun and its orbiting bodies) and other important links with the sun (solar energy, for example).

4 When students have completed their inquiries and comments about the items on the transparency, turn off the overhead. Instruct the students to turn their paper over and *note* what they now *know* about the cue word. One variation is to have them write a definition for the concept. What they write can be

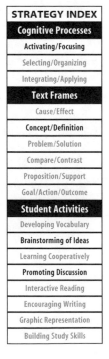

STRATEGY INDEX
Cognitive Processes
Activating/Focusing
Selecting/Organizing
Integrating/Applying
Text Frames
Cause/Effect
Concept/Definition
Problem/Solution
Compare/Contrast
Proposition/Support
Goal/Action/Outcome
Student Activities
Developing Vocabulary
Brainstorming of Ideas
Learning Cooperatively
Promoting Discussion
Interactive Reading
Encouraging Writing
Graphic Representation
Building Study Skills

"Solar System" LINK

Darth Vader   craters
                                              galaxy
          stars   solar panels

astronaut
                                              sun
          Star Wars

Jupiter   outer space
                                              Voyageur
          solarium

Mars   astroid
                                              moons

solar cells   **Solar System**
                                              rings
                                                    Saturn

space ship   planets
          orbit

meteorites   gravity   Milky Way

                                              life
solar energy   telescope   comets

                                              Star Trek
satellite
          Martians

based on both their prior experience and the class dis-cussion during the inquiry.

5 Students are now ready to read the passage. After reading, they may be asked to note what they now know after they've encountered new material.

ADVANTAGES

LINK offers a number of advantages as a teaching strategy:

- Students become "warmed up" to the material and anticipate the content based on what they already know.

- All students are actively involved in the process and contribute to the class listing of associations.

- Students are given practice in assuming the responsibility for raising questions, seeking clarifi-cations, and engaging in discussion about the topic.

- This strategy is appropriate for students in all grade levels and is adaptable to all content areas.

FURTHER RESOURCES

Cook, D. (Ed.). (1989). *Strategic learning in the content areas.* Madison, WI: Department of Public Instruction.

Vaughan, J., & Estes, T. (1986). *Reading and rea-soning beyond the primary grades.* Boston, MA: Allyn and Bacon.

Magnet Summaries

Consider, for a moment, President Clinton's recent proposal for universal health care in America. It was packaged in a mammoth document, and crammed with information relating to health-care providers, insurance companies, "managed competition," costs of services and pharmaceuticals, "core benefits," and many other aspects pertaining to health care. What sense could we make out of all this? How could we cut to the essence of what this program might mean to us?

We rely on summarization—those distillations by various experts, analysts, and writers, and by ourselves—which makes a bulk of information manage-

---

We are virtually bombarded by information that needs to be summarized in order to be digested.

---

able for understanding. As adults, both on the job and during the other aspects of our daily lives, we are virtually bombarded by information that needs to be summarized in order to be digested.

Summarization skills are also critical for our students, many of whom find it very difficult to reduce information into its essential ideas in order to learn it. Lack of summarization skills results in many of our students not being able to "see the forest for the trees" as they read. The Magnet Summary (Buehl, 1993) is a strategy that helps students rise above the details and construct meaningful summaries in their own words.

THE STRATEGY

Magnet Summaries involve the identification of key terms or concepts—magnet words—from a reading. Students then use these magnet words to organize important information that should be included in a summary. Using this strategy with students consists of the following steps:

1 Introduce the idea of "magnet words" to the students. Begin by inquiring what effect a magnet

has on metal. Just as magnets attract metal to them, magnet words attract information to them. Instruct students to read a short portion of their text assignment, looking for a key term or concept that the details in the passage seems to "stick" to. When they have finished reading, solicit possible magnet words from the students. Comment that most of the information in the section is connected to the magnet word. Note that magnet words frequently appear in titles or headings or may be highlighted in the text in bold or italic print. Caution, however, that all words in bold or italic are not necessarily magnet words.

2 Next, write the magnet word on the chalkboard or overhead transparency. Ask the students to recall some of the important details from the passage that are connected to the magnet word. As you write these items around the magnet word, have the students follow the same procedure on a 3"x5" card. Allow the students a second look at the passage to include any important details which may have been missed (see example of History magnet word cards).

3 The students are now ready to complete their reading of the entire text passage. Distribute three to four additional 3"x5" cards to each student for recording the magnet words from the remaining material. For younger students, indicate that they should identify a magnet word for each paragraph or section following a heading.

4 In cooperative groups, have the students decide upon the best magnet words for the remaining cards. Then have them generate the important details for each magnet word. When the groups are finished, each student will have four to five cards, each with a magnet word and key related information.

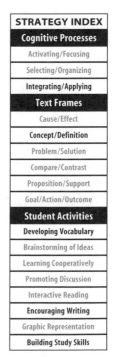

STRATEGY INDEX
Cognitive Processes
Activating/Focusing
Selecting/Organizing
Integrating/Applying
Text Frames
Cause/Effect
Concept/Definition
Problem/Solution
Compare/Contrast
Proposition/Support
Goal/Action/Outcome
Student Activities
Developing Vocabulary
Brainstorming of Ideas
Learning Cooperatively
Promoting Discussion
Interactive Reading
Encouraging Writing
Graphic Representation
Building Study Skills

Magnet Summaries in History

160 Acres	farm for 5 years
Homestead Act	
Congress	
many went West	1862

"Many people went west because of the <u>Homestead Act</u>*, which gave 160 acres to people if they farmed them for 5 years."*

insects	The Great Plains
	drought
Hardship	
hot/cold weather	crops failed

"In the Great Plains, people had <u>hardships</u> *with the very hot and very cold weather, and their crops failed due to drought and insects."*

way they plowed	dug wells
wheat	
Dry Farming	
	irrigation
windmills	

"Farmers needed to do <u>dry farming</u>*, so they dug wells, made windmills, and changed the way they plowed to grow wheat."*

no trees	far from each other
loneliness	
Homes on the Prairie	
	dirt floors
sod houses	"soddies"

"<u>Homes on the Prairie</u> *were sod houses, called 'soddies,' because they had no trees. People were lonely because the houses were far from each other."*

5 Next model for the students how the information on one of the cards can be organized and combined into a sentence that sums up that passage of the text. The magnet word should occupy a central place in the sentence. Note that some of the details may not be as important as others and will be omitted from the sentence.

Have students return to their cooperative groups and construct a sentence which summarizes each of their remaining cards. Urge students to try to combine the information into one sentence, although on occasion it may be necessary to come up with two sentences for a particular card. Have them work out their sentences on scratch paper first. Then the final version of each sentence is written on the back of the appropriate card, and the magnet words are underlined. (See examples of sentences below the History magnet cards.)

6 Finally, direct the students to arrange the sentences in the order they wish their summary to read. At this point, the sentences will need to be altered so they flow smoothly from one to the other. Model inserting connectives and other language that integrates the sentences into a summary. At this point students should also judge whether all important ideas are included, and whether anything further can be deleted. Students then test their summaries by listening to how they sound when they are read aloud.

The following Magnet Summary for a history passage on Life in Great Plains in the 1880's is an example:

*Many people went west because of the **Homestead Act**, which gave 160 acres to people if they farmed them for 5 years. But in the Great Plains, people had **hardships** from the very hot and very cold weather, and their crops failed due to drought and insects. Therefore farmers needed to do **dry farming**, so they dug wells, made windmills, and changed the way they plowed to grow wheat. The farmers' **homes on the prairie** were sod houses, called 'soddies,' because there were no trees. The people were lonely because the houses were far from each other.*

ADVANTAGES

Magnet Summaries help students with the difficult task of condensing and organizing information. The strategy offers several advantages:

- Students gain practice in translating key concepts into their own words.

- Students flesh out their understandings of key vocabulary and ideas.

- Students learn to identify main ideas and relate significant information to these ideas.

- Students are actively involved in constructing a meaningful synthesis of what they have read.

- This strategy is appropriate for students from elementary age through high school and can be successfully used with materials in all content areas.

FURTHER RESOURCES

Buehl, D. (December, 1989). Magnetized: Students are drawn to technique that identifies key words. *WEAC News & Views*, 13.

Hayes, D. (November, 1989). Helping students GRASP the knack of writing summaries. *Journal of Reading*, 96-101.

Vacca, R., & Vacca, J. (1993). *Content area reading* (4th ed.). New York, NY: Harper Collins College Publishers.

Point-of-View Study Guides

"Excuse me, but what do you think about…?" It seems that we live in an age when people's points of view are being almost continuously solicited. Public opinion polls, radio call-in shows, "Sound Off" columns in the local newspapers, "man-in-street" interviews, telephone surveys—all are attempts by someone to find out what we think.

The Point-of-View Study Guide (Wood, 1988) is a strategy that capitalizes on this interest in examining things from other perspectives. Students read a selection, not as themselves, but as if they were a character involved in the events of the reading. The process of reading becomes more "personalized," as students add information from their "role" into their understanding of the text. The Point-of-View Study Guide follows an interview format, and encourages students to respond in their own words to the ideas and information in the reading.

THE STRATEGY

Point-of-View Study Guides can be constructed for a wide variety of situations, from literature to science selections. Using this strategy involves the following steps.

1 Identify an appropriate role or character for a selection that students have already read. To model the point-of-view strategy for students, assume this role yourself. Ask the students to interview you by having them generate meaningful questions that could be answered by information in the text. For example, following a reading about explorers to the New World, you could be interviewed as a Native American of that time. Or following a selection on endangered species, you could be interviewed as a whale.

2 Next, choose an appropriate role or character for a new selection. Create a series of interview questions that will help the students focus on the important elements of the text. Distribute these questions as the study guide for the selection. Students reading the novel *Bridge to Terabithia* by Katherine

Patterson could be asked to comment on events at the end of the book from the perspective of Leslie, the girl who had died. Students reading a history passage on immigration could be asked to read from the perspective on a specific immigrant (see social studies example). Students reading a biology selection on roots could answer interview questions that assume they are a taproot (see Science example).

Students read a selection, not as themselves, but as if they were a character involved in the events of the reading.

---

3 As the students read, have them look for information that will enable them to respond to the interview questions. Interview responses should be written in **first person** and should be elaborated upon using specific material from the reading. The written responses should read as dialogue, not as typical answers to questions in the text. For example, a student response to a question of an Italian immigrant regarding difficulties of life in America might be:

We have not been accepted by many Americans. We have encountered prejudice because of our different languages and customs. We also have had to work in jobs with long hours and low wages, and some of us have experienced acts of violence. Some of us are accused of being anarchists or socialists, and are treated as if we are a threat to the government.

STRATEGY INDEX

Cognitive Processes
Activating/Focusing
Selecting/Organizing
Integrating/Applying

Text Frames
Cause/Effect
Concept/Definition
Problem/Solution
Compare/Contrast
Proposition/Support
Goal/Action/Outcome

Student Activities
Developing Vocabulary
Brainstorming of Ideas
Learning Cooperatively
Promoting Discussion
Interactive Reading
Encouraging Writing
Graphic Representation
Building Study Skills

4 As the students become comfortable with point-of-view guides, they will be able to create their own interview questions. Assign a role, and have

Point-of-View Study Guide

(Social Studies Example)

Chapter 5: "The Age of Industry"

You are about to be interviewed as if you were a person living in the United States in the mid to late 1800's. Respond to the following interview questions as if you were an…

Italian Immigrant

Waves of Immigration (p. 111) and *New Immigrants* (p. 111)

1. During what time period did most of your fellow Italian immigrants come to the United States?
2. What made you decide to leave Italy?
3. When you landed in New York, you met immigrants from many other countries. What countries were they from and what were some of their reasons for coming to the United States?

Immigrant Life (p. 114) and *Nativist Feelings* (p. 115)

4. What types of employment did you have to choose from when you landed in America?
5. Why do some of you immigrants object to the process of "assimilation"?
6. Have you encountered any difficulties being an immigrant in the United States. What kinds of problems have you and your fellow immigrants experienced?

Limiting Immigration (p. 116)

7. As an immigrant, what are your feelings toward legislation to limit immigration? Would you support or oppose such legislation?

Point-of-View Study Guide

(Science Example)

Chapter 23: "Roots and Stems"

You are about to be interviewed as if you were a part of a plant. Respond to the following questions as if you were a...

Taproot

Root Systems (p. 385)

1. What plant are you a taproot for? What other plants have taproots such as yourself?
2. We notice that some plants have fibrous root systems. How are you different from these roots?
3. Not to get personal, but all you roots seem rather hairy. Why do you roots have those hairy growths?

Primary Root Tissues (p. 387) and *Secondary Growth in Roots* (p. 387)

4. Could you take a couple of moments and describe how you grow?
5. Roots must need to be tough when growing through the soil. What enables you to push through the soil?

students work in pairs. One student reads the selection as that character, and the partner reads as the interviewer. The interviewer's job during reading is to formulate questions to be posed to the character. Following the reading, the students can participate in an actual mock interview, or the questions and their responses can be collected as a written exercise.

Students develop sensitivity to different perspectives of events and ideas.

ADVANTAGES

Point-of-View Study Guides offer a number of advantages for use with students:

- The guides help students to become more personally engaged in the reading, and help bring material "to life."

- Students gain practice in translating the language of the text into their own words and they are engaged in a more in-depth processing of the material.

- Students are encouraged to draw upon their own experiences to understand events in the text, and they are asked to elaborate upon the information in a meaningful way.

- Students develop sensitivity to different perspectives of events and ideas.

- This strategy can be effectively used with materials in all content areas. It is especially effective with social studies and literature.

FURTHER RESOURCES

Wood, K. (1988). Guiding students through informational text. *The Reading Teacher, 41*(9), 912-920.

Wood, K., Lapp, D., & Flood, J. (1992) *Guiding readers through text: A review of study guides.* Newark, DE: International Reading Association.

Possible Sentences

In the days before fax machines, when the telegram was the best way to quickly contact someone, it was recognized that key words can communicate the gist of a message. Suppose you had received a telegram that contained only the following words: "hepatitis A, outbreak, gourmet restaurants, Chicago, epidemic, health inspector, quarantine, incubation period, viral, liver." Do you think you could piece together the probable meaning?

In all likelihood, you would be able to draw upon your background experiences and knowledge to construct a prediction for the entire message: "There is an

---

Reading becomes an exercise in discovering the accuracy of predictions about key terms.

---

outbreak of hepatitis A in Chicago. Health inspectors have quarantined some gourmet restaurants associated with the outbreak. Hepatitis A has an incubation period before it appears and is a viral disease which affects the liver."

Possible Sentences (Moore and Moore, 1986) is a strategy that helps students process the key vocabulary of a passage before they began reading. It encourages students to make predictions about the probable meaning of the passage based on what they know, or can anticipate, about a number of key terms. Then when the students begin reading, they have already previewed some of the major ideas of the text. Their reading becomes an exercise in discovering the accuracy of their predictions about the key terms.

THE STRATEGY

Possible Sentences is a strategy that can be implemented with a wide variety of materials. Using this strategy involves the following steps.

1 Identify ten to fifteen key concepts or terms from the material the students will be reading. Include both terms which will be familiar to the students as well as some which might prove to be obstacles to their reading.

List these on the chalkboard or on an overhead transparency. For example, the key terms from a social studies textbook passage on ancient Greece might include: "Hellenic Age, architecture, Parthenon, Plato, philosophy, theater, democracy, and *The Republic*."

2 Next, ask the students to select at least two of the terms and include them in a sentence that could possibly appear in the reading. You are basically asking them to predict how the terms might be used in the passage. Elicit a sentence from the class and write it exactly as given on the chalkboard. Underline the key words. Then ask for a second sentence which uses different terms. Continue until all the words from your list are represented in sentences on the board. For those terms that are unfamiliar to them, encourage the students to guess at a probable meaning.

For a passage on the ancient Greeks, for example, some students might know that "The Parthenon was a temple with many statues." They may also feel confident offering that "The ancient Greeks did a lot with architecture, philosophy, and the arts." They may not know exactly who Plato and Aristotle were, so hunches based on the key terms would have to be followed. (See Social Studies Possible Sentences.)

3 Students are now ready to read the passage and check the accuracy of their possible sentences. Students evaluate each possible sentence in terms of whether it is *true* (the text backs up their prediction), *false* (the text presents a different use of the term), or *don't know* (the statement can be neither proved nor disproved based on the text).

For example, some of the possible sentences on ancient Greece were directly contradicted by the text. Aristotle was

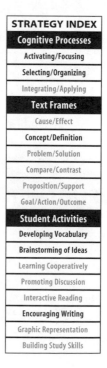

STRATEGY INDEX
Cognitive Processes
Activating/Focusing
Selecting/Organizing
Integrating/Applying
Text Frames
Cause/Effect
Concept/Definition
Problem/Solution
Compare/Contrast
Proposition/Support
Goal/Action/Outcome
Student Activities
Developing Vocabulary
Brainstorming of Ideas
Learning Cooperatively
Promoting Discussion
Interactive Reading
Encouraging Writing
Graphic Representation
Building Study Skills

Possible Sentences

(Social Studies Example)

Chapter 4: "Greek Culture"

Key Terms

Hellenic Age	Plato
architecture	philosophy
Parthenon	*The Republic*
democracy	theater
tragedies	Aristotle
the arts	statues
temple	Father of Biology

Possible Sentences

DK   1. The <u>Hellenic Age</u> was a time of many <u>tragedies</u>.

T   2. The ancient Greeks did a lot with <u>architecture,</u> <u>philosophy,</u> and <u>the arts</u>.

T   3. The <u>Parthenon</u> was a <u>temple</u> with many <u>statues</u>.

F   4. The Greeks had a <u>democracy</u> and their government was called <u>*The Republic*</u>.

F   5. <u>Plato</u> was called the <u>Father of Biology</u>.

DK   6. Greek <u>theater</u> performed plays by <u>Aristotle</u>.

the Father of Biology, and *The Republic* was a work by Plato, not the name of the Greek government. Others were not clearly dealt with in the text. Many of Aristotle's activities were detailed, but any connection with Greek theater was not mentioned. Tragedies were discussed as a form of theater, but the book did not mention whether this time in history was also a time of tragedy.

4 When the students have completed reading the passage and evaluating the possible sentences, work with the class to determine how any could be changed to be more consistent with the reading. Have the students locate the relevant portions of the text which elaborate on the individual terms as a means for defending their corrections. Students may find that some statements need to be expanded into two or three sentences in order to accurately reflect the text. Students may also generate entire new sentences to added to the original group.

The Possible Sentences for the passage on ancient Greece may be altered by the students to now read:

- *The **Hellenic Age** was a time of great achievement in **architecture**, **philosophy**, and **the arts**.*

- *Greek **theater** featured **tragedies** and comedies.*

- *The **Parthenon** was a **temple** with many **statues**. The Parthenon was an important example of Greek **architecture**.*

- *The Greeks were the first people to develop a **democracy**.*

- ***Aristotle** was called the **Father of Biology**.*

- ***Aristotle** and **Plato** were famous for philosophy. Plato wrote **The Republic**.*

5 Possible Sentences is an excellent strategy to organize for students to complete in cooperative groups. As students become familiar with this process, they will be able generate, evaluate, and revise their own Possible Sentences as a cooperative group activity. Provide each group with the list of key terms and have them complete each step of the process as a cooperative activity.

ADVANTAGES

Possible Sentences is an effective strategy for a number of reasons:

- Students become acquainted with the key terms and vocabulary of a passage *before* they begin to read.

- Students are engaged in an exercise that has them actively predicting the major ideas of the material.

- Students are involved in a process that helps them to establish their purposes for reading.

- Students activate some of what they know about the information before they read, and they are able to share their background knowledge with their classmates.

- This strategy is appropriate for students from elementary age to high school. Possible Sentences is a strategy that can be effectively used with materials in all content areas.

FURTHER RESOURCES

Moore, D., & Moore, S. (1986). *Possible sentences.* In E. Dishner, T. Bean, J. Readence & D. Moore (Eds.), *Reading in the content areas: Improving classroom instruction* (2nd ed.). Dubuque, IA: Kendall/Hunt.

Moore, D., Readence, J., & Rickelman, R. (1989). *Prereading activities for content area reading and learning* (2nd ed.). Newark, DE: International Reading Association.

PReP— Prereading Plan

The background knowledge students bring to the classroom greatly determines how successful they will be in learning new material. Researchers argue that a student's prior knowledge accounts for more variation in comprehension than either IQ or reading achievement. Students in today's classrooms bring a wide disparity of knowledge and experiences to any specific learning situation. How can the teacher find out what students know about a topic and assess whether they know enough to understand what will be taught?

The key is to work with students before they read a passage so that what they know is brought out into the open and is connected to what they will be learning. One effective strategy for preparing students to learn new material is PReP (Prereading Plan) (Langer, 1984).

THE STRATEGY

PReP is a three-step process that teachers use before asking students to read a passage, view a film, and otherwise learn new material.

1 The teacher selects a key concept or vocabulary term from the reading and works with the students on a free association exercise. "Tell me what you think of when you hear the word *gravity*." The teacher writes the student responses on the chalkboard, overhead transparency, or chart paper. All responses are listed and students are not allowed to comment on their responses. *Force, apple, pull, weight, float, sun, space ship, fall down*—all might be associations offered by your students during this phase.

Work with students before they read so that what they know is brought out into the open and is connected to what they will be learning.

---

2 When all students have responded, the teacher selects some of the responses and asks for clari-

fication from the students who offered them. "What made you think of *airplane crash? Astronaut? Earth spinning? Newton?*" This process allows students to share knowledge with the entire class and helps them to reflect on what they know about this concept.

One student may note that she remembers learning that the earth spins around the sun because of gravitational pull. Another recalls the story of Isaac Newton under the apple tree. A third talks about astronauts who experience weightlessness when they have left the earth's gravity.

3 The teacher provides time for students to continue to reformulate their ideas about the concept. "Based on our discussion, do you have any further ideas about *gravity*?"

The clarification phase will jog students' memories, making them aware of things they knew about the topic. This step will give them a chance to offer these thoughts to the class. These are added to the associations listed on the chalkboard and students are allowed to elaborate on their contributions.

4 The students are now ready to read a science passage which deals with gravity.

ADVANTAGES

PReP offers a number of advantages as a teaching strategy:

- The major concepts to be learned are identified ahead of time so students know what to look for when they read.

- Students have a chance to explore useful information they know about the topic before they started reading.

- Students with little background knowledge about the

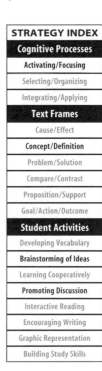

STRATEGY INDEX
Cognitive Processes
Activating/Focusing
Selecting/Organizing
Integrating/Applying
Text Frames
Cause/Effect
Concept/Definition
Problem/Solution
Compare/Contrast
Proposition/Support
Goal/Action/Outcome
Student Activities
Developing Vocabulary
Brainstorming of Ideas
Learning Cooperatively
Promoting Discussion
Interactive Reading
Encouraging Writing
Graphic Representation
Building Study Skills

topic have the opportunity to build their information base through the class discussion before having to struggle with the reading.

- Students are more likely to be motivated to read a passage that relates to something they already know.

FURTHER RESOURCES

Langer, J. (1984). Examining background knowledge and text comprehension, *Reading Research Quarterly, 19*.

Cook, D. (Ed.). (1989). *Strategic learning in the content areas.* Madison, WI: Department of Public Instruction.

Problematic Situations

*H*ow did the Egyptians build the pyramids? What did people use for medicines before there were commercial drugs? What would happen if you put too much yeast in a bread recipe? What would you expect the countryside to look like after a glacier has melted? How did stone-age hunters kill large animals like Woolly Mammoths? What would you do if somebody has threatened to beat you up after school?

Children are never at a loss for questions and from a young age on, many of these queries focus on "how" or "what." Tapping into this natural curiosity is an excellent way to prepare students for reading material that deals with problems and solutions. Problematic Situations (Vacca and Vacca, 1993) is a strategy that presents students with a circumstance that is subsequently developed or explained in a reading selection.

Before reading the passage, the students first brainstorm possible solutions to or results of the problematic situation. This process activates what the stu-

---

Tapping into natural curiosity is an excellent way to prepare students for reading material that deals with problems and solutions.

---

dents already know about the situation and helps them to focus their attention on the key elements of the text as they read. Problematic Situations also increase motivation for reading, as students want to find out whether their solutions will be confirmed by the author.

THE STRATEGY

Problematic Situations can be used to prepare students for any type of reading material that deals with a problem/solution relationship. Using the strategy with students involves the following steps:

1 Examine the reading assignment and develop a problematic situation for the students to consider. Provide the students with enough of the relevant information about the situation so that they will be able to focus their attention on the key ideas in the passage as they read. It is especially important that the context of the problem be clearly defined.

For example, the following problematic solution may be created for students reading the short story *The Most Dangerous Game* by Richard Connell:

> *A man is trapped on a small island covered with jungle vegetation. He has a three hour head start on someone who is trying to kill him. The killer is well-armed but the man has only a knife. The killer will be pursuing the man with hunting dogs. What could this man do to try to save himself?*

2 Next, pose the problematic situation to the students and in cooperative groups have them generate possible results or solutions. Have each group record all their responses as they discuss them. When they have listed their responses have them discuss *why* each is appropriate or "would work." For example, students preparing to read a passage on nutrition and how different nutrients affect the body might be given the following problematic situation:

> *You are the head coach of the Chicago Bears football team. Two players come to you for advice about what foods they should be eating to stay in the best shape for playing their position. One is a linebacker, the other is the huge lineman William "The Refrigerator" Perry. What suggestions would you give each of them?*

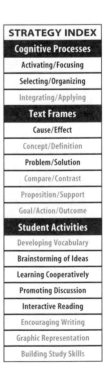

STRATEGY INDEX
Cognitive Processes
Activating/Focusing
Selecting/Organizing
Integrating/Applying
Text Frames
Cause/Effect
Concept/Definition
Problem/Solution
Compare/Contrast
Proposition/Support
Goal/Action/Outcome
Student Activities
Developing Vocabulary
Brainstorming of Ideas
Learning Cooperatively
Promoting Discussion
Interactive Reading
Encouraging Writing
Graphic Representation
Building Study Skills

Students might list foods like the following for the linebacker: steak, potatoes, vegetables, pasta, milk. Their reasoning might be that the linebacker needs to be tough but also fast and will burn up a lot of energy on the field. The students realize that "The Refrigerator" needs to watch his weight, so they decide he should eat vegetables, salads, fruits, and avoid fatty foods like pizza or french fries.

3 With some problematic solutions, it may be desirable to have each group decide upon their most promising result or solution. As part of their deliberations, have them develop their justification for why their decision might be considered the best answer. Each group then presents their solutions to the entire class for discussion.

For example, students discussing possible actions for *The Most Dangerous Game* Problematic Situation will have to consider which of the solutions—from planning various ambushes to setting a variety of traps—would be most conceivable and likely to succeed. Students preparing to read a selection about the Pilgrims and their religious beliefs would need to decide what course of action might work best for the following Problematic Solution:

> *A group of very religious people is living in a country where they cannot worship freely. They feel that the laws of the country and the government are against them. Other people in this country attack their beliefs and this religious group feels persecuted. What can they do to solve their problem?*

4 The students are now ready to test their solutions by reading the selection. Instruct students to add to or modify their solutions as they gain more information from the text. Students reading the nutrition selection may realize that "The Refrigerator" could also eat lean meats as part of his diet, and that he should be careful of how many carbohydrates he consumes. Students reading *The Most Dangerous Game* may discover that the hunted man, Rainsford, unsuccessfully tries some of their ideas as he struggles to outwit his adversary. Students may discover that the Pilgrims attempted several of their solutions before embarking to the American continent to create a new society.

5 How did the student predictions compare with the information provided in the text? As a final step, revisit the original Problematic Situation and solicit any revisions, additions, or further comments students may have now that they have read the selection. Open the discussion to consider whether some of the student options might be better solutions than those presented by the author.

ADVANTAGES

Problematic Situations help launch students into successfully analyzing material that deals with "how" or "what" relationships. The strategy achieves a number of benefits for students:

- Students have an opportunity to "take stock" of things they already know which relate to ideas in the reading.

- Students find that their curiosity is piqued and they are more motivated to tackle a reading that will answer some of their questions.

- Students anticipate the problem-solving frame of mind that they will need to assume when reading.

- Students consciously connect new information to their questions about problematic situations.

- This strategy can be used with a wide variety of materials in all subject areas, and is appropriate for students at all levels, from elementary age through high school.

FURTHER RESOURCES

Vacca, R. & Vacca, J. (1993). *Content area reading* (4th ed.). New York, NY: Harper Collins College Publishers.

Proposition/Support Outlines

Imagine that you are reading the latest George Will column in *Newsweek* Magazine. Or an editorial in the morning newspaper. Or a review of a recent movie, a new book, or a local restaurant. Each of these different texts represents a style of writing that features a proposition which is discussed and supported. The propositions vary: "Newt Gingrich is a highly effective politician." "The proposed school bond referendum should be passed." *Interview With the Vampire* is an entertaining movie that does not measure up to the novel." "The food served at La Ritz is expensive but outstanding."

The statements vary, but your frame of mind when reading this style of writing remains the same. You ask yourself, "What proposition is being offered, and is the support for the proposition convincing?"

Proposition/Support Outlines help students become critical readers of material that presents viewpoints, opinions, debatable assertions, theories, or hypotheses. Proposition/Support writing places a special premium on analytical thinking abilities, which many students find especially challenging. It is no accident that many of the questions students face on SAT and ACT tests target author's point of view and supporting argumentation. Proposition/Support Outlines supply students with a framework for analyzing the types of justification an author supplies to support a proposition.

THE STRATEGY

Proposition/Support Outlines work in a variety of contexts. Using this strategy involves the following steps.

1 Initiate with students a discussion of the difference between "facts" and "opinions." Brainstorm with students a definition of each and generate a list of examples of "facts" and "opinions." "The Milwaukee Brewers lead the league in stolen bases" is a fact statement. "The Milwaukee Brewers play exciting baseball" is an opinion that may or may not be supported by facts. "The earth's rain forests are shrinking" is a fact statement. "The loss of our rain forests will

lead to an environmental disaster" is an opinion—in this case a hypothesis—that may or may not be supported by facts.

2 Introduce the term "proposition"—a statement that can be argued as true. Provide students with several possible propositions: "Wisconsin is America's dairyland." "The Brewers need a power hitter to win their division." "Cats make the best pets." "The park needs new playground equipment." "Today's movies are too violent." Divide students into cooperative groups and assign each group the task of generating as many arguments as they can that might be used to support one of these propositions.

Proposition/Support Outlines help students become critical readers of viewpoints, opinions, debatable assertions, theories, or hypotheses.

---

3 In large group sharing, help students categorize the types of arguments that could be used to support a proposition. Introduce a blank Proposition/Support Outline on an overhead transparency, and model with students how support for a proposition could be categorized as facts, statistics, examples, expert authority, and logic and reasoning.

4 Assign a text that follows a Proposition/Support frame of writing and have students complete the Proposition/Support Outline as they analyze the author's arguments. Select for student practice a text that features a clear proposition. Initially, it may be desirable to have students work in pairs to identify the proposition, and then share how they used the clues in the text to determine it.

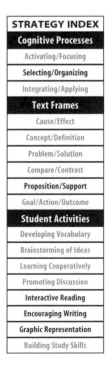

STRATEGY INDEX
Cognitive Processes
Activating/Focusing
Selecting/Organizing
Integrating/Applying
Text Frames
Cause/Effect
Concept/Definition
Problem/Solution
Compare/Contrast
Proposition/Support
Goal/Action/Outcome
Student Activities
Developing Vocabulary
Brainstorming of Ideas
Learning Cooperatively
Promoting Discussion
Interactive Reading
Encouraging Writing
Graphic Representation
Building Study Skills

Rain Forests Proposition/Support Outline

Proposition:

> *The loss of our rain forests will lead to an environmental disaster.*

Support:

1. Facts

- *Rain forests use up Carbon Dioxide.*
- *There is increased Carbon Dioxide in the earth's atmosphere.*
- *The rain forests contain many endangered plant and animal species.*
- *Deforestation leads to widespread soil erosion in many areas*
- *The burning of fossil fuels puts Carbon Dioxide into the environment.*

2. Statistics

- *The 1980's were the "hottest" decade in the last 100 years.*
- *One acre of tropical forest disappears every second.*
- *4 million acres (larger than the state of Connecticut) disappear every year.*
- *50 to 100 species are destroyed with each acre of forest cleared.*
- *If present trends continue, half of the rain forests of Honduras and Nicaragua will disappear by year 2000.*

3. Examples

- *India has almost no remaining rain forest.*
- *Current plans target eliminating much of the Congo's rain forest.*
- *Run-off from deforestation in Indonesia threatens their coral reefs and diminishes the fish population.*
- *Cutting of rain forests in Bangledash and the Philippines has led to killer floods.*

4. Expert Authority

- *Computers predict doubling of Carbon Dioxide in the next century, raising temperatures 3 to 9 degrees.*
- *National Center for Atmospheric Research believes increased Carbon Dioxide will lead to Greenhouse Effect and global warming.*
- *Environmentalist Expert Al Gore calls Greenhouse Effect our most serious threat ever.*

5. Logic and Reasoning

- *Warmer temperatures will harm crops and increase energy costs.*
- *More people will starve because of less food and increased population growth.*
- *The polar glaciers will melt and raise the sea level, flooding coastlines.*
- *Many species useful to humans will disappear.*
- *More sections of the world will become unhabitable deserts due to soil loss, from erosion, overgrazing, and overcultivation.*

Students then use the outline to categorize the arguments supporting the proposition. For example, an article on rain forests might contain information and arguments that are reflected in all five support categories (see Rain Forest Proposition/Support Outline).

5 How convincing is the supporting argumentation? Analyze with students the types of support presented? Does an author rely almost solely on logic and reasoning and examples, neglecting to use statistics or other facts? Is only a single expert authority cited? How reliable are the statistics? (For example, public survey results are statistics which might change frequently.) Do the examples seem to be typical or atypical? Has important counteracting information been omitted from the discussion?

6 As students become confident using Proposition/Support Outlines, they may be asked to use them in a variety of contexts. Students may be asked to investigate different propositions possible from a textbook passage. For example, some members of the class may read a passage on the Mexican War to locate support for the proposition: "Santa Anna was looking out for the best interests of the Mexican people." Other students could be asked to defend the proposition: "The Americans had good reasons for wishing to expand their borders to the southwest."

The Proposition/Support Outline is also an excellent guide for independent research, as it provides students with a framework for examining reference materials for relevant information and arguments.

ADVANTAGES

Proposition/Support Outlines offer a number of advantages for use with students:

- The outlines provide students with practice in developing critical reading skills.

- Students learn to identify propositional writing and analyze supporting arguments.

- Completed outlines help focus class discussions or debates, and they provide structure for writing assignments, such as position papers or independent research.

- This strategy is especially useful with "issues-related" text, and with language arts and social studies materials.

FURTHER RESOURCES

Buehl, D. (September, 1992). Outline helps students analyze credibility of author's premise. *WEAC News & Views*, 8.

Cook, D. (Ed.). (1989). *Strategic learning in the content areas.* Madison, WI: Department of Public Instruction.

Santa, C. (1988). *Content reading including study systems: Reading, writing and studying across the curriculum.* Dubuque, IA: Kendall/Hunt Publishing Company.

The Pyramid Diagram

Visualize the following setting. A corporate meeting room of a major company, with a table surrounded by a score of executives, each responsible for delivering a report. What follows is a parade of statistics, an array of colorful charts and computer graphics, and a pile of data. But what sense is to be made from all this information? Clearly, that is the point of the meeting, to understand the implications of the information so that important decisions can be made.

Students need to sort through information to draw conclusions and make observations.

As a critical part of their daily reading demands, students also need to sort through information to draw conclusions and make observations. Yet national studies of reading achievement consistently indicate that students have much more difficulty making inferences than identifying facts. The Pyramid Diagram (Solon, 1980) is a strategy that guides students in selecting appropriate information from a reading so that it can be analyzed and conclusions can be made.

THE STRATEGY

The Pyramid Diagram engages students in both reading and writing activities. Using this strategy involves the following steps.

1 Provide students with a focusing question which will help them select relevant information from their reading. For example, a focusing question for students reading a selection about Benjamin Franklin might be "What were Ben Franklin's accomplishments during his life?" A focusing question for students reading a passage on hurricanes might be "What are the problems caused by hurricanes?"

2 Distribute 3"x5" cards to the students and have them read the selection. As they read, they should use the cards for recording information that deals with the focusing question. One piece of information is recorded on each card. Students looking for Franklin's achievements might write "invented the lightning rod" on one card and "was ambassador to France" on a second card. They would continue making cards until they completed reading the passage.

3 Model the process of categorizing the information selected from the reading by soliciting student responses from their cards. Write each response on a 5"x 8" index card and line the cards along the chalkboard tray in the order given. Next ask the students if any of the cards can be grouped together. Allow discussion and recognize disagreements as the students determine how the cards might be categorized. Move the cards to reflect the class consensus, thus forming the "foundation layer" of the pyramid diagram (see Ben Franklin Pyramid Diagram example).

4 Next ask students to brainstorm possible category headings for each grouping of cards. Again allow discussion and help the class reach a consensus. Write the labels selected for each group on new cards and tape them as a second layer of the pyramid, above the corresponding categories. For example, students might decide on the label "statesman" or "leader" for the cards detailing Franklin's roles as delegate to the Constitutional Convention and diplomat to France. Several of Franklin's other accomplishments could fall under the category of "inventor." Students may also decide that he was a writer and a scientist after they consider the information on the other cards.

5 On the chalkboard, draw two rectangles representing the top two layers of the pyramid. Ask students to determine an appropriate title for the pyramid.

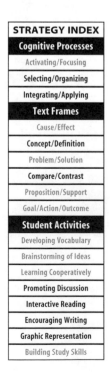

STRATEGY INDEX
Cognitive Processes
Activating/Focusing
Selecting/Organizing
Integrating/Applying
Text Frames
Cause/Effect
Concept/Definition
Problem/Solution
Compare/Contrast
Proposition/Support
Goal/Action/Outcome
Student Activities
Developing Vocabulary
Brainstorming of Ideas
Learning Cooperatively
Promoting Discussion
Interactive Reading
Encouraging Writing
Graphic Representation
Building Study Skills

Pyramid Diagram for Benjamin Franklin

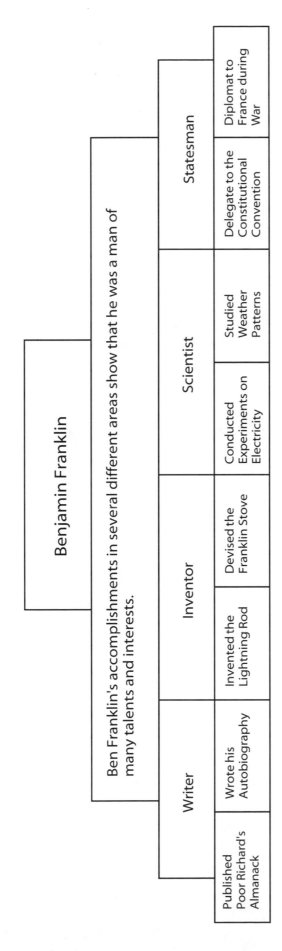

Benjamin Franklin

Ben Franklin's accomplishments in several different areas show that he was a man of many talents and interests.

Writer		Inventor		Scientist		Statesman	
Published Poor Richard's Almanack	Wrote his Autobiography	Invented the Lightning Rod	Devised the Franklin Stove	Conducted Experiments on Electricity	Studied Weather Patterns	Delegate to the Constitutional Convention	Diplomat to France during War

This title is placed in the top rectangle. Then, using the title, the category labels, and the details from the reading, have each student write a one sentence statement which summarizes the information represented in the pyramid.

For example, after constructing a Ben Franklin pyramid, students might conclude:

> *Ben Franklin's accomplishments in several different areas show that he was a man of many talents and interests.*

6 Students are now prepared to write a one paragraph conclusion that addresses the focusing question. The second layer of the pyramid provides them with a topic sentence. The third layer suggests subsequent sentences which will expand on the topic sentence. And the bottom layer identifies appropriate details which may be used to illustrate each of these examples.

> *Benjamin Franklin's accomplishments in several different areas show that he was a man of many talents and interests. Franklin was a well-known writer who published the popular Poor Richard's Almanack and wrote his autobiography. As an inventor, he is responsible for inventing the lightning rod and Franklin stove. He also was a scientist who conducted experiments on electricity and studied weather patterns. Finally, Franklin was an important statesman who served as a delegate to the Constitutional Convention and as a diplomat to France during the Revolutionary War.*

7 Once students have become comfortable with using pyramid diagrams, these steps may be undertaken in cooperative groups. Students first read the selection and complete their cards, and then meet to construct the rest of the pyramid as a group. Students could then write their one paragraph conclusions as individuals or as a group collaboration.

ADVANTAGES

Pyramid Diagrams offer a number of advantages for use with students:

- Students are involved in constructing a visual representation of how important details can be used to draw conclusions and make observations.

- Students are directive in their reading so that they actively search for appropriate information from a selection.

- Students gain practice in writing well-organized summaries of text.

- This strategy can be adapted for use from elementary through secondary levels, and is appropriate for all content areas.

FURTHER RESOURCES

Kinkead, D., Thompson, R., Wright, C., & Gutierrez, C. (1992). Pyramiding: Reading and writing to learn social studies. *The Exchange. Secondary Reading Interest Group Newsletter, 5*(2).

Solon, C. (1980). The pyramid diagram: A college study skills tool. *Journal of Reading, 23*(7).

RAFT— Role/Audience/Format/Topic

We know that writing is an important way to help students think about what they have read. But teachers are often frustrated with the quality of writing completed by students. We receive writing that is woefully short, lacking in detail, poorly organized, bereft of imagination, and carelessly thrown together. Students tend to view writing as a laborious task in which they have no personal investment. As a result, the advantages of using writing as a tool for learning are sometimes defeated.

The RAFT strategy (Santa, 1988) is one technique that attempts to address teacher concerns with student writing. Developed in the Montana Writing Project, RAFT is a method that works to infuse imagination, creativity, and motivation into a writing assignment. RAFT involves writing from a viewpoint other than that of a student, to an audience other than the teacher, in a form other than a standard theme or written answers to questions.

THE STRATEGY

RAFT is an acronym which stands for:

R — Role of the writer (Who are you?)
A — Audience for the writer (To whom are you writing?)
F — Format of the writing (What form will your writing assume?)
T — Topic to be addressed in the writing (What are you writing about?)

The RAFT strategy involves the following steps:

1 Analyze the important ideas or information that you want students to learn from reading a story, a textbook passage, or other material. Consider how a writing assignment will help to consolidate this learning. How might student writing help students remember the stages of the digestive system? Or understand the frustrations of the American colonists? Or empathize with the emotions of one of the characters in a story? This establishes the *topic* for the writing.

2 Brainstorm possible *roles* students could assume in their writing. For example, students in a science class could imagine they were a French Fry that was describing what was happening to it during each stage of the digestive process. Students studying the colonial period in American history could assume the role of a colonist upset with more taxes. Students in Language Arts reading the book *James and the Giant Peach* by Roald Dahl could be assigned the role of James, who needs to tell somebody about how his malevolent aunts are treating him.

RAFT involves writing from a viewpoint other than that of a student, to an audience other than the teacher, in a form other than a standard theme or written answers to questions.

---

3 Next decide who the *audience* will be for this communication and determine the *format* for the writing. For example, the French Fry could be writing in the format of a travel journal, to be read by other French Fries headed toward the digestive system. The colonist could be writing in the form of a petition intended for other outraged colonists. James could be writing a letter to state adoption authorities complaining of his ill treatment.

4 After students have completed the reading, write RAFT on the chalkboard and list the role, audience, format, and topic for the writing. All students could be assigned the same role for their writing, or you may offer several different roles from which students could choose. For instance, after reading a passage

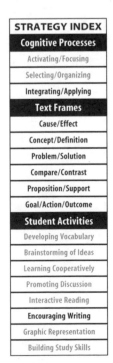

Examples of RAFT Assignments

Role	Audience	Format	Topic
Newspaper Reporter	Readers in the 1870s	Obituary	Qualities of General Custer
Lawyer	U.S Supreme Court	Appeal Speech	Dred Scott Decision
Abraham Lincoln	Dear Abbey	Advice Column	Problems with his Generals
Mike Royko	Public	News Column	Capital Punishment
Frontier Woman	Self	Diary	Hardships in West
Constituent	U.S. Senator	Letter	Gun Control
Newswriter	Public	News Release	Ozone Layer has been formed
Chemist	Chemical Company	Instructions	Combinations to Avoid
Wheat Thin	Other Wheat Thins	Travel Guide	Journey through the Digestive System
Plant	Sun	Thank You Note	Sun's role in Plant's Growth
Scientist	Charles Darwin	Letter	Refute a Point in Evolution Theory
Square Root	Whole Number	Love Letter	Explain Relationship
Repeating Decimal	Set of Rational Numbers	Petition	Prove You Belong to this Set
Cook	Other Cooks	Recipe	Alcoholism
Julia Child	TV Audience	Script	Wonders of Eggs
Advertiser	TV Audience	Public Service Announcement	Importance of Fruit
Lungs	Cigarettes	Complaint	Effects of Smoking
Huck Finn	Jim	Letter	What I learned During the Trip
Joseph Stalin	George Orwell	Letter	Reactions to *Animal Farm*
Comma	9th Grade Students	Complaint	How is Misused
Trout	Self	Diary	Effects of Acid Rain on Lake

on soil erosion, students could write from the perspective of a farmer, a fish in a nearby stream, a corn plant, or a worm in the topsoil. Students could be given the choice of several characters in a story to represent their role for writing.

ADVANTAGES

The RAFT strategy offers a number of advantages to the classroom teacher:

- Students are forced to process information rather than merely write out answers to questions.

- Students are given a clear structure for their writing. They know what point of view to assume and they are provided with an organizational scheme. Furthermore, the purpose of the writing is clearly outlined.

- Students are more motivated to undertake the writing assignment because it attempts to involve them personally and allows for more creative responses to learning the material.

- RAFT is a strategy adaptable to all content areas, including science, social studies, and math.

FURTHER RESOURCES

Cook, D. (Ed.). (1989). *Strategic learning in the content areas.* Madison, WI: Department of Public Instruction.

Santa, C. (1988). *Content reading including study systems.* Dubuque, IA: Kendall/Hunt.

Save the Last Word for Me

For many students, "reading" means taking a quick and superficial trip through the text for the sole purpose of answering assigned questions. Unfortunately, these students often never achieve more than a very cursory literal level treatment of what they have to read. Classroom discussions which encourage students to think about what they have read tend to sputter as a result, because students did not engage in reflective reading behavior.

**Save the Last Word for Me
is an excellent strategy
to use with material that may
elicit differing opinions
or multiple interpretations.**

Activities that stimulate students to reflect upon what they read help to develop active and thoughtful readers. One effective strategy for developing readers who are thinkers is Save the Last Word for Me (Vaughan and Estes, 1986). Devised by Burke and Harste, Save the Last Word both prompts students to actively interact with the text and provides an cooperative group format for the subsequent class discussion.

THE STRATEGY

Save the Last Word for Me is an excellent strategy to use with material that may elicit differing opinions or multiple interpretations. The strategy involves the following steps:

1 Assign the story, selection, or passage to be read. As students read the material, they are required to locate five statements that interest them or that they would like to say something about. These might be statements with which they agree or disagree, or statements that contradict something they thought they knew. They could also be statements that particularly surprised, excited, or intrigued them. With literature, students could also select revealing statements or actions made by characters in the story.

Students place a light check mark in pencil next to their five chosen statements.

2 Distribute five index cards to each student, a card for each of their selected statements. Students write one of the statements on the front side of a card. On the reverse side of the card, students write the comments they wish to make about that statement.

For example, a student reading a selection about wolves as an endangered species might select this statement for the front of a card: "Wolves are sometimes illegally shot by ranchers who fear that their livestock will be attacked." The student may write the following comment on the back of the card: "Ranchers ought to have a right to protect their animals from dangerous predators like wolves."

3 Divide the class into small groups of four to five members. All students in each group are allowed to share one of their five designated statements with their group members. The first student reads a statement to the group and helps them locate the statement in the text. However, the student is not allowed to make any comments on the statement until the other members of the group give their reactions or responses. In effect, the student gets "the last word" in the discussion of this statement.

For example, one student might share the statement: "Wolves naturally try to avoid contact with humans." But she cannot discuss her comments— that people's fears of wolves are exaggerated, especially because of the way wolves are treated in fairy tales—until every other group member has had a say about this statement. The attitude during this phase is: "Here is a statement that interested me. You tell me what you think, and then I will tell you what I think."

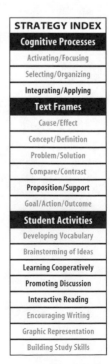

STRATEGY INDEX
Cognitive Processes
Activating/Focusing
Selecting/Organizing
Integrating/Applying
Text Frames
Cause/Effect
Concept/Definition
Problem/Solution
Compare/Contrast
Proposition/Support
Goal/Action/Outcome
Student Activities
Developing Vocabulary
Brainstorming of Ideas
Learning Cooperatively
Promoting Discussion
Interactive Reading
Encouraging Writing
Graphic Representation
Building Study Skills

Save the Last Word for Me

1. As you read, make a check mark (√) in pencil next to five statements that you:

   • agree with;
   • disagree with;
   • or want to say something about.

2. After you finish reading, write each statement on the front of a separate 3"x 5" card.

3. On the back of each card, write the comment you would like to share with your group about each statement.

4. When you meet in your group:

   a. Select a member of your group to go first.

   b. This person reads the statement from the front of one of his or her cards, but is <u>not allowed to make any other comment</u>.

   c. Every other member of the group talks about the statement and makes comments.

   d. When everyone else is done talking, then the person who wrote the card can make comments.

   e. Go on to a second student and repeat the process until all the cards are shared.

4 With the completion of the discussion of the first statement, the attention goes on to a second student, who is asked to share a different statement, without comment, until all other students have spoken. This process continues until everyone in the group has shared one statement and has provided the "last word" in the discussion.

ADVANTAGES

Save the Last Word for Me offers a number of advantages as a teaching strategy:

- Students are given an exercise which requires them to adopt a more reflective stance as they read.

- Students are encouraged to talk about things in the reading that personally connected to them and they all have an opportunity to participate in the class discussion on the reading.

- Students are allowed to hear their classmates' views before they offer their own. This provides students with the chance to adjust their comments and reflect upon their ideas before having to express them to others.

- This strategy is adaptable to most subject areas and is appropriate for elementary through high school age students.

FURTHER RESOURCES

Vaughan, J., & Estes, T. (1986). *Reading and reasoning beyond the primary grades*. Boston, MA: Allyn and Bacon.

Science Connection Overview

For many students, reading science materials is often like reading a foreign language. They encounter many unfamiliar words which have precise meanings in the language of science. Many of these new terms are used only rarely outside a science context. Science readings also tend to contain very detailed information through which students have a difficult time maneuvering. A persistent problem for students when reading science is their inability to make connections between the science in their books and their understandings of the world around them.

The Connection Overview (Buehl, 1992) is a pre-reading strategy that can help students make these connections. The strategy involves examining a sci-

---

Discuss with students how science helps them to understand some aspect of their lives or world.

---

ence chapter or article before reading it in order to link the content with something the student already knows or has experienced. Before students become immersed in the details of the reading, they are thus able to "see the big picture" of how this chapter will relate to some part of the world around them.

THE STRATEGY

The Connection Overview strategy involves the following steps:

1 Introduce the exercise by discussing with students how science helps them to understand some aspect of their lives or world. Select several examples of science material and elicit from the class how each can be connected to their lives. A passage on cold and warm fronts and the resulting rain? Students might connect to why rain occurs when it does, or why it is often colder after it rains. A chapter on microorganisms that live in water? Students might connect by reflecting why it is unsafe to drink lake or river water. An article on endangered plants and animals?

Students might connect to news stories on the Amazon jungle or dolphins captured in tuna nets.

2 Distribute a blank Connection Overview to students and model with the overhead projector how it use it. Tell students to follow along as you skim a portion of the reading and think aloud about things mentioned in the text that you know or with which you are familiar. Ignore technical terms or information that seems unfamiliar. For example, an overview of a Biology chapter on fungi would pass over terms like "basidiomycota," "multinucleate," and "zygospore" and would instead focus on things that are familiar: "mushrooms," "bread mold," "yeast," and "Dutch Elm disease."

3 Assign students to work in pairs to complete the *What's Familiar* section of the Connection Overview (see Biology example). Emphasize that only familiar, nontechnical information should be gleaned from their surveying and skimming of the chapter. Encourage them to use the pictures and graphics in the chapter to assist them in making connections.

For example, students doing an overview of the Biology fungi chapter would likely discover that even though the text contains a lot of forbidding terminology, there is much that connects to their lives and experiences. Most students would recognize many of the mushrooms, lichens, and molds featured in chapter photographs.

4 If the chapter has a summary, direct students to read it over to look for key topic areas that seem to be covered in the chapter. For example, the summary for the Biology fungi chapter indicates that three general areas appear to be addressed: how fungi are structured, how they reproduce, and how they feed. These are entered in the *What Topics are Covered* section of the overview.

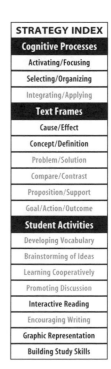

STRATEGY INDEX
Cognitive Processes
Activating/Focusing
Selecting/Organizing
Integrating/Applying
Text Frames
Cause/Effect
Concept/Definition
Problem/Solution
Compare/Contrast
Proposition/Support
Goal/Action/Outcome
Student Activities
Developing Vocabulary
Brainstorming of Ideas
Learning Cooperatively
Promoting Discussion
Interactive Reading
Encouraging Writing
Graphic Representation
Building Study Skills

Connection Overview: Biology

What's Familiar?	What's the Connection? Skim & Survey the Chapter for things that are familiar and connect with your life or world. List them below: • *mushrooms* • *fungi on rotting plants* • *mold on spoiled food* • *lichens* • *spores* • *penicillin* • *yeasts* • *Dutch Elm disease* • *plant rusts*
What topics are covered?	Read the Summary. What topic areas seem to be the most important? • *how they look or are structured* • *how they reproduce* • *how they feed and stay alive*
What questions do you have?	Questions of Interest. What questions do you have about this material that may be answered in the chapter? • *Why do mushrooms grow in damp places?* • *Why does food get moldy when it spoils?* • *Why do they put yeast in bread when they bake it?* • *Why are some mushrooms poisonous?* • *How can you tell which mushrooms are poisonous and which are safe?* • *What do fungi eat?* • *Does the medicine penicillin come from a fungus?*

How is it organized?	Chapter Organization: What categories of information are provided in this chapter?
	
	• *Structure of Fungi*
	• *Nutrition*
	• *Reproduction*
	• *Variety of Fungi:* molds *imperfect*
	          yeasts
	          mushrooms
	          lichens

Translate	Read and Translate: Use 3x5 Cards for Vocabulary.

 © 1995 Wisconsin State Reading Association, Doug Buehl, *Classroom Strategies for Interactive Learning*

5 The students are now ready to generate some personal questions they may have about the material. Encourage students to think about what they know in this topic area and what they might want to find out. These are entered in the *What Questions Do You Have* section. Questions generated from the fungi chapter might be: Why do mushrooms grow where they do? Why are some mushrooms poisonous? Why do they put yeast in bread? Why does food get moldy?

6 Will the students' questions receive answers in the reading? Students next complete the *How is it Organized* portion of the Connection Overview by outlining the chapter organization. Categories on information are usually signaled by headings or section titles. The fungi chapter was organized into four sections: structure, nutrition, reproduction, and variety of fungi.

7 Students are now prepared to read the passage. As they read, they will have their Connection Overview available as a resource to remind them of what this chapter is about as they encounter the technical vocabulary and detailed information. As students read, have them use index cards to translate technical terms into more understandable language (see "rhizoid" example). This step reinforces that the point of reading science is to make connections.

ADVANTAGES

The Connection Overview strategy offers a number of advantages to the classroom teacher of science:

- Students make meaningful connections with the material before they are asked to process unfamiliar information.

- Students see how the information fits together, and have a construct for making sense of what they read.

- Students are provided with a structure for translating difficult material into something that they can make sense to them.

- This strategy may be adapted for use with elementary age children through high school age students.

FURTHER RESOURCES

Buehl, D. (Spring, 1992). The connection overview: A strategy for learning in science. *WSRA Journal*, 21-30.

Front of Card

rhizoid

Back of Card

little fibers that grow out of a bread mold

they are like roots and they hook the mold onto the bread or other food

Semantic Feature Analysis

It is well established that vocabulary knowledge is a key predictor of how well a student will comprehend a given text. But developing vocabulary knowledge involves much more than merely learning dictionary definitions of words. Students need vocabulary instruction that helps them to broaden their understanding of concepts and to differentiate between related or similar words.

The Semantic Feature Analysis strategy (Johnson and Pearson, 1984) is a technique that guides students

---

Students have a visual reminder of how various concepts are alike and different.

---

through analyzing vocabulary by identifying key characteristics and comparing these characteristics with other known concepts. Through use of a matrix grid, students are able to code a number of key vocabulary or concepts in terms of several important qualities. When they have completed a semantic feature matrix, students have for reference a visual reminder of how various concepts are alike and different.

THE STRATEGY

Semantic Feature Analysis involves the following steps:

1 Select from your instruction a category of concepts to be analyzed. Younger students will respond better to more concrete concepts such as *farm animals, vegetables, sports,* or *musical instruments.* As students become more experienced, abstract categories such as *forms of government, character traits,* or *geometric forms* can be analyzed with this strategy.

2 List several terms within this category in the left column of the Semantic Feature Matrix (see People in Government example). These words should be familiar to the students. For example, words within the category of *farm animals* might include *cow, dog,*

cat, chicken, pig, horse. Words within the category of people in government might include *President, Senator, Judge,* and *Governor.*

3 Next list three or four key features (traits, properties, or characteristics) that these words share. Features for farm animals may include: "has fur," "has feathers," "can be house pet," "makes food," "is used for meat." Features for government officials may include: "elective position," "passes laws," "has limits on service," "serves the entire country."

4 Students are now ready to code each feature in terms of whether the targeted words typically possess that feature. A plus sign (+) is entered if the word exhibits that feature; a minus sign (–) is entered if the word does not exhibit that feature. A question mark can be entered if students are not sure.

For example, students completing a Semantic Features Analysis of the Governor of Wisconsin would place pluses in features such as "is an elective office," "has term length," "can be held by any legal voter," "vetoes laws," "administers laws," and "works within the U.S." An analysis of the role of a U.S. senator might lead to minuses in features such as "is an appointive office," "has limits on service," and "can be held by any legal voter." Students might place a question mark in the feature of "serves the entire U.S." for it could be argued that a senator serves the state he or she represents, but may also have a national perspective.

5 The semantic feature matrix is now ready to accommodate more terms within the selected category and more features to be analyzed. Ask students to offer additional words and features which may be included in the matrix. Other governmental officials suggested by students could be members of the cabinet, state legislature, or city council.

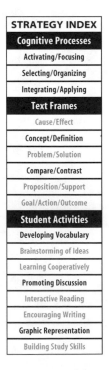

Semantic Feature Analysis: People in Government

Category: People in Government

Features	is an elective office	is an appointive office	has term lengths	has limits on service	can be held by any legal voter	passes laws	vetoes laws	administers laws	declares laws unconstitutional	serves the entire U.S.	works within the U.S.
President of U.S.	+	-	+	+	-	-	+	+	-	+	+
Governor of Wisconsin	+	-	+	-	+	-	+	+	-	-	+
U.S. Senator	+	-	+	-	-	+	-	-	-	?	+
Secretary of Defense	-	+	-	-	+	-	-	+	-	+	+
Supreme Court Justice	-	+	-	-	+	-	-	-	+	+	+
Ambassador to England	-	+	-	-	+	-	-	?	-	+	-
Wis. Assembly Member	+	-	+	-	+	+	-	-	-	-	+

Other features might focus on terms in office or jurisdiction of service. These additional elements are then coded with plus or minus signs, or question marks.

6 Examine the matrix and discuss similarities and differences between the terms for the category. Guide the students in developing generalizations about how each word is unique from other related concepts. If two words have exactly the same pattern of pluses and minuses, challenge the students to identify a feature that will differentiate between the two.

ADVANTAGES

Semantic Feature Analysis offers a number of advantages to the classroom teacher:

- Students began to analyze key vocabulary as concepts rather than as short definitions.

- Students become aware of relationships between words within a specific category, and they develop sensitivity for how these words are similar and how they are different.

- A Semantic Feature Matrix can be continually expanded and refined during a unit of study. As students learn new information or encounter new concepts, these can be added to the matrix.

- A matrix provides an excellent summary of a unit and review for exams. The matrix also presents students with organized information for writing assignments.

- Semantic Feature Analysis is a strategy adaptable to all grade levels and all content areas, including science, social studies, and math.

FURTHER RESOURCES

Johnson, D., & Pearson, P. (1984). *Teaching reading vocabulary* (2nd ed.). New York, NY: Holt, Rinehart, & Winston.

Pittelman, S., Heimlich, J., Berglund, R., & French, M. (1991). *Semantic feature analysis: Classroom applications.* Newark, DE: International Reading Association.

SMART—Self-Monitoring Approach to Reading and Thinking

What is it about effective readers that sets them apart from students who struggle with reading? One major difference is that effective readers carry on an internal monologue while they read. It is as if effective readers operate with a split personality. One personality is hard at work with the task at hand—reading a textbook chapter for instance. This is the personality concerned with cognitive activities such as selecting what's important in that chapter, organizing this information in conjunction with what is already known, and preparing to answer a series of questions on the material. It is this personality that gets most of our attention as teachers. We are able to observe the student at work and assess the results. This is the student we see sitting at a desk, interacting with print.

But it is a second personality that separates effective from less effective readers. This second personality works in the background, directing and evaluating all those cognitive activities needed to success-

---

Effective readers carry on an internal monologue while they read.

---

fully learn. This personality represents that "inner voice" that issues commands during reading: "Slow down! This is pretty tough going!" "Hold it here! This doesn't make any sense. Better reread." or "This stuff doesn't look very important. I'll just skim quickly over it and get into the next section." Effective learners talk to themselves.

Researchers call this internal monologue *metacognition*—the ability to think about your thinking. Metacognition involves a self-awareness of what one is doing and how it is going. It also reflects an ability to switch gears and try something else when things break down, such as when a reading passage is proving particularly difficult. Ineffective readers approach print passively and continue to plow ahead, even if nothing is making sense. But ineffective readers can also be taught how to activate the control center in their minds that directs their learning.

One strategy that triggers students to think about how their reading is proceeding is SMART (Vaughan and Estes, 1986). SMART is an acronym for A Self-Monitoring Approach to Reading and Thinking.

THE STRATEGY

SMART is based on the premise that successful reading begins with recognizing what you did and did not understand from a passage. The strategy involves the following steps:

1 Select a passage of four or five paragraphs that you can use to model how you think as you read. Ask the students to follow along as you think aloud about your reading. It may help to enlarge the passage and place it on an overhead transparency. After reading a couple of sentences or a paragraph, comment aloud that you understand this section and make a check mark (√) in the margin. Continue on, and model a part that seems confusing to you. Write a "?" next to this sentence or paragraph. Note to the students that here is something you do not fully understand.

2 When you have finished the entire passage, model how you can paraphrase the material in your own words so that it makes sense to you.

3 Then take a second look at each "?" you recorded in the margin. Brainstorm with the students what you could do to make sense of those parts too. Observe that some of the "?" may now make sense after you have read the entire passage. Change them to check marks. Then list and discuss the students' suggestions for dealing with the remaining question marks.

4 Introduce the SMART protocol to students (see "Read SMART" graphic). Model the troubleshooting steps with the passage you are modeling and have the students help you as they use their books. Emphasize that there are strategies you can

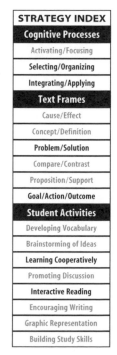

STRATEGY INDEX
Cognitive Processes
Activating/Focusing
Selecting/Organizing
Integrating/Applying
Text Frames
Cause/Effect
Concept/Definition
Problem/Solution
Compare/Contrast
Proposition/Support
Goal/Action/Outcome
Student Activities
Developing Vocabulary
Brainstorming of Ideas
Learning Cooperatively
Promoting Discussion
Interactive Reading
Encouraging Writing
Graphic Representation
Building Study Skills

Read SMART!

1. **Read.** Read a section of the text. With a pencil lightly place a "√" next to each paragraph that you <u>understand</u>. Place a "?" next to each paragraph that has something you do <u>not understand</u>.

2. **Self-Translate.** At the end of each section, stop and explain to yourself what you read, *in your own words*. You can <u>look back</u> at the text as you go over the material.

3. **Troubleshoot.** Go back to each "?" you have made. Try to see if you can now make sense of this paragraph.

   a. **Re-read** the trouble spot to see if it now makes sense. If it still does not make sense:

   b. **Pinpoint** the problem by figuring out <u>why</u> you are having trouble:

      • Is it a difficult word or unfamiliar vocabulary?
      • Is it a difficult sentence or confusing language?
      • Is it about things you know very little about?

   c. **Try** a Fix-Up Strategy.

      • Use the Glossary or some other Vocabulary Aid.
      • Look over the Pictures or other Graphics.
      • Examine other parts of the Chapter (Summary, Review Section, Diagrams, Other Features)

   d. **Explain** to yourself exactly <u>what</u> you do not understand or are confused about.

   e. **Get Help.** Ask the teacher or a classmate.

try before you need to ask for help, and that successful reading means that you clear up each "?"

5 Now have the students read a passage on their own, using the check mark and question mark system. As the students finish, have them work through the SMART protocol with a partner, verbalizing what they understood and didn't understand, and working together through any problems in understanding. Emphasize that before asking for help, students should be able to: (1) specify the source of their problem (an unfamiliar word, an unclear sentence, a need for more examples, etc.); and (2) explain what they did to try to solve their problem.

ADVANTAGES

SMART offers a number of advantages as a teaching strategy:

- Students are provided with a system that helps them actively monitor their reading success.

- Students learn to verbalize what they do and do not understand in a reading.

- Students are encouraged not to be satisfied until an entire reading makes sense, and they are given specific steps to try to clear up trouble spots.

- Students become involved in putting the material into their own words, thus helping them to remember as well as understand it

- This strategy is adaptable to most subject areas and is appropriate for elementary through high school age students. It is especially effective in cooperative group or tutorial settings.

FURTHER RESOURCES

Vaughan, J., & Estes, T. (1986). *Reading and reasoning beyond the primary grades*. Boston, MA: Allyn and Bacon.

Story Mapping

"*Once upon a time…*" "*Could you please read me a story, Dad?*" "*Did you hear the story about the ice fisherman who…*" "*You'll never believe what happened last night! Let me tell you the whole story…*"

Stories—we grew up hearing them as children. We read them throughout our schooling. We enjoy reading them now for pleasure. We experience them on television and in movie theaters, and we tell them to our friends. Much of the way we view the world around us has been organized into stories.

Story Maps feature graphic representations of key story elements.

Children encounter narrative text very early in their lives, and they begin to internalize the common elements found in most stories. Story Mapping (Beck and McKeown, 1981) is a strategy that helps students use their knowledge of narrative structure to analyze stories. Story Maps feature graphic representations of key story elements. The resulting visual outline helps students build a coherent framework for understanding and remembering a story.

THE STRATEGY

Story Maps can be created for both short stories and longer works, such as novels. Using the strategy with students involves the following steps:

1 Reinforce with students the key elements of a story. For example, introduce story structure by posing the following question: "I'm going to read you a story. What would you want to know about this story?" Students would likely comment that they would like to know who the story is about, what happens in the story, where the story takes place, and how the story ends.

These common elements of narrative structure can be presented as a "story star" on an overhead transparency. Note how each of these questions can be reworded to reflect the basic elements of a story. "Who" refers to characters, "where" and "when" involve setting and mood, "what happens" details events of the plot, "how did it end" involves the resolution of the story's conflict. "Why" questions get at the author's theme of the story (see Story Star example).

2 Next, read to the students a story that you have selected for its clear illustration of story structure. When you have finished the story, hand out blank story maps to each student. Have them fill in the key information from the story as you model this process on an overhead transparency. Emphasize the recording of only major events—those which move the plot along—and establish the "initiating event" that sets the story into motion. As a part of this process, review the basic kinds of conflict: within a person, between people, between people and nature.

For example, students reading the Stephen King short story *Battleground* first identify the characters (the hired killer Renshaw, and the tiny soldiers), and the setting (Renshaw's San Francisco apartment). They note that the action is initiated by the arrival of the box of miniature soldiers to Renshaw's apartment, and they record the other major events, leading to the climax, when Renshaw attacks his tiny assailants from the ledge outside his window. Subsequent action includes the explosion, Renshaw's death, and the onlookers' discovery of the message about the scale model atomic bomb which had arrived, unbeknownst to Renshaw, with the tiny soldiers. Students identify the conflict as between people, and note that it is resolved with Renshaw's death (see "Battleground" Story Map example).

3 Model with students how to use the organized information in the story map to determine the author's theme.

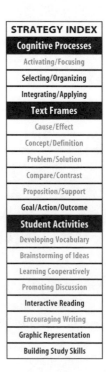

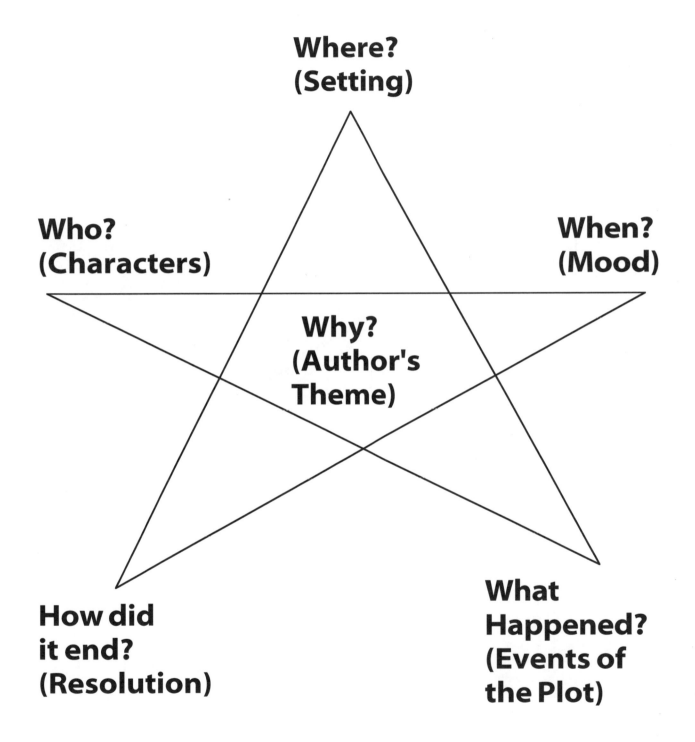

Where?
(Setting)

Who?
(Characters)

When?
(Mood)

Why?
(Author's
Theme)

How did
it end?
(Resolution)

What
Happened?
(Events of
the Plot)

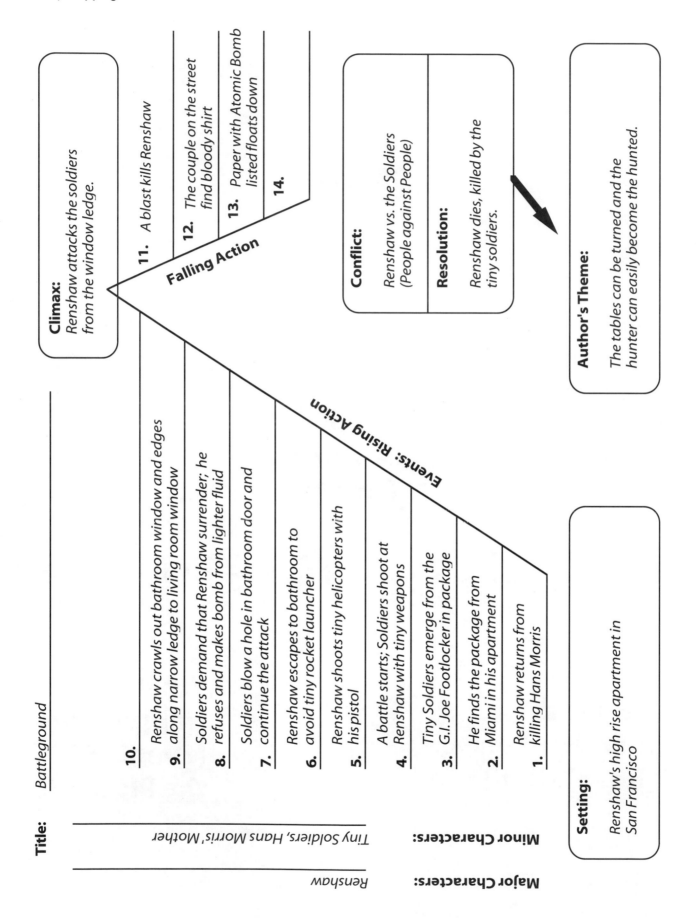

Title: _____

Battleground

Climax:
Renshaw attacks the soldiers from the window ledge.

11. A blast kills Renshaw

Falling Action

12. The couple on the street find bloody shirt

13. Paper with Atomic Bomb listed floats down

14.

10.

9. Renshaw crawls out bathroom window and edges along narrow ledge to living room window

8. Soldiers demand that Renshaw surrender; he refuses and makes bomb from lighter fluid

7. Soldiers blow a hole in bathroom door and continue the attack

6. Renshaw escapes to bathroom to avoid tiny rocket launcher

5. Renshaw shoots tiny helicopters with his pistol

4. A battle starts; Soldiers shoot at Renshaw with tiny weapons

3. Tiny Soldiers emerge from the G.I. Joe Footlocker in package

2. He finds the package from Miami in his apartment

1. Renshaw returns from killing Hans Morris

Events: Rising Action

Conflict:
Renshaw vs. the Soldiers (People against People)

Resolution:
Renshaw dies, killed by the tiny soldiers.

Author's Theme:
The tables can be turned and the hunter can easily become the hunted.

Setting:
Renshaw's high rise apartment in San Francisco

Minor Characters:
Tiny Soldiers, Hans Morris, Mother

Major Characters:
Renshaw

Emphasize that the conflict and the way it is resolved provides a great deal of insight into the point the author was making in the story.

Students will recognize in the short story *Battleground* that the tables are turned on the major character. Renshaw is a hired killer who "gets his due." Students might articulate the theme as "What goes around comes around," or "The hunter can easily become the hunted," or "Those who live by violence die by violence."

4 Demonstrate how the key questions to be asked about a story conform to the structure displayed in the story map. Significant questions should relate to the roles played by the setting, character develop-

---

Students become practiced in using story structure as a basis for the creation of their own stories.

---

ment, events of the plot, conflict and its resolution, and the author's theme in the telling of the story. Questions may also focus on the author's craft, such as the use of language and literary devices, in developing the story's components.

For example, questions for *Battleground* might highlight the irony of a wily killer being outwitted by someone he has victimized. Questions about specific events in the rising action could establish how Renshaw's mood changed from annoyance to anger to desperation.

5 The students are now ready to use the story map to analyze a short story that they read on their own. After their reading, have the students work with a partner to complete the story map. As a whole group, solicit possible statements of the author's theme and discuss the rationale for each based on information from the story.

ADVANTAGES

Story Maps contribute to student learning in a number of ways:

- Students are provided with a visual framework for understanding and analyzing stories, and their knowledge of story structure is reinforced as a foundation for the successful reading of narrative text.

- Questions for guiding and discussing stories that are derived from the elements of story structure lead to more coherent and integrated comprehension from students. Students improve their ability to predict probable questions for a particular story.

- Students become practiced in using story structure as a basis for the creation of their own stories. Students also have a clear model for the writing of summaries and other reactions to the stories they read.

- This strategy is appropriate for most narrative text. It can be modified for use with students at all levels, from elementary age through high school.

FURTHER RESOURCES

Beck, I., & McKeown, M. (November/December, 1981). Developing questions that promote comprehension: The story map. *Language Arts*, 913-918.

Structured Notetaking

"Make sure that you take notes on this!" This oft-heard directive is delivered by teachers almost daily—to students learning from print, from classroom presentations and discussions, and from video. Teachers know that notetaking is a prerequisite for remembering and learning, and that it is an essential study strategy.

Yet teachers are frequently disappointed with the results of student notetaking. Student notes often are disorganized and lack important information. Students are frequently confused as to what to write

---

Structured Notetaking involves creating graphic outlines that serve as organized study guides for students as they take their notes.

---

down and what to leave out. And some students may associate notetaking with mindlessly copying material verbatim from a book, from the chalkboard, or from an overhead transparency. The result may be a notebook that has lots of writing in it but is ineffective as a resource for study.

Structured Notetaking (Smith and Tompkins, 1988) is a strategy that guides students toward taking more effective notes. The strategy makes use of graphic organizers, a powerful means of representing ideas and information. Graphic organizers provide students with a visual framework for making decisions on what should be included in their notes, and they impose a structure on student notes that make them useful for future referral. Structured Notetaking is an excellent strategy to use in all aspects of classroom learning where notetaking is desirable—from printed materials, from video, from teacher presentations, and from class or group discussions.

THE STRATEGY

Structured Notetaking involves creating graphic outlines that serve as organized study guides for students

as they take their notes. Eventually students will be able to devise their own structured notes as an independent study skill. Using Structured Notetaking in the classroom consists of the following steps.

1 Preview the material the students will be learning. Identify the organizational frame of the material. The following six organizational frames address the most common ways of organizing information (see discussion of "Text Frames" in Chapter 2):

- *Problem/Solution*
- *Compare/Contrast*
- *Cause/Effect*
- *Proposition/Support*
- *Goal/Action/Outcome*
- *Concept/Definition*

2 Next, create a graphic organizer that follows the organizational frame you have identified. The graphic organizer will be distributed to students as a notetaking "study guide"—they take notes by recording relevant information in the appropriate spaces in the graphic outline.

For example, a selection about endangered animals may follow a problem/solution organizational frame. Students would be provided with "Endangered Animals" graphic outlines to be completed with their notes from the reading (see "Endangered Animals" Structured Notes example). The first endangered animal they encounter could be the "Dolphin." As they read about the dolphin, students then select information that fits into the four boxes in the graphic: *"dolphins get caught in underwater tuna nets," "commercial*

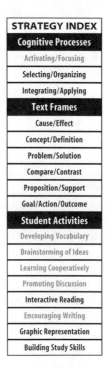

STRATEGY INDEX
Cognitive Processes
Activating/Focusing
Selecting/Organizing
Integrating/Applying
Text Frames
Cause/Effect
Concept/Definition
Problem/Solution
Compare/Contrast
Proposition/Support
Goal/Action/Outcome
Student Activities
Developing Vocabulary
Brainstorming of Ideas
Learning Cooperatively
Promoting Discussion
Interactive Reading
Encouraging Writing
Graphic Representation
Building Study Skills

Structured Notetaking in Science: Endangered Animals

What kind of problem is this animal having?

Dolphins are being caught in underwater tuna nets and are being killed.

Who or what is causing the problem?

Commercial fisheries who use this type of underwater net to catch tuna.

Write the name of an Endangered Animal Here:

The Dolphin

Where does this animal live?

Dolphins live in deep sea waters in the Atlantic Ocean and Mediterranean Sea.

What can be done to help this animal?

We can buy tuna that is marked "dolphin-safe."
We can write letters to government leaders for international fishing controls.

North to Chicago: Structured Notes from Video

Life in the South Before Migration North

- Many lived in Shacks
- Poor Food
- Segregation
- Low Wages
- Few Jobs
- Jim Crow Laws
- KKK Harassment
- Poor Schools
- Second Class Status
- Discrimination
- Bo Weevil ruined Cotton
- Racial Violence
- Lack of Protection from Courts & Law

Factors Which Encouraged Black Americans to Move North to Chicago

- Recruited to north by factories needing laborers
- Were provided with free transportation (railroads)
- Agents sent south enouraged African Americans to come north
- World War I caused need for workers and brought about new jobs & new factories
- New laws restricted immigration from other countries
- The Chicago Defender newspaper spoke to African Americans
- Hangings & lynchings were increasing in the south

Life in Chicago for Black Americans

- Last hired, first fired
- Had jobs but little money
- Postwar depression put people out of work
- Created neighborhoods of all African Americans
- Housing shortages
- Culture flourished— music, food, churches
- African American city
- African American business leaders and business leaders emerged
- Competed for jobs with returning WWI soldiers
- Race riots, bombs, killings

fisheries are causing the problem," "we can buy tuna with the 'dolphin-safe' designation," and *"we can lobby for international fishing regulations."*

The students then go on and complete a second graphic organizer for the next endangered animal.

3 Before students began completing the structured notes, discuss the specific organizational frame being followed. Highlight the text frame each time you provide structured notes so that students began to recognize these organizational frames.

4 Structured Notetaking provides a number of opportunities for students to collaborate on their notetaking. When structured notetaking is first introduced to students, have them work in pairs while reading a passage. As part of this process, students justify to their partners their decisions on what to select and where to place it in the graphic outline.

For example, students viewing a video program on the migration of African Americans from the rural South to northern cities in the early 20th Century would be provided with a graphic organizer that involves both cause/effect and compare/contrast text frames (see the "North to Chicago" example). As stu-

---

As students gain practice in using structured notes, they will begin to develop their own graphic organizers to structure their notes.

---

dents view the video, they individually record information which first describes life in the rural South and then life in Chicago. They are also cued into looking for the causal factors which encouraged the movement north. Students are instructed to write quickly and not to worry about legibility and completeness.

When the video is over, put students in pairs or in small groups and give them a second copy of the graphic organizer. They then compare their notes from the video with their classmates and develop a more thorough set of structured notes. These can be then photocopied for each member of the group.

5 As students gain practice in using structured notes, they will begin to develop their own graphic organizers to structure their notes. At first, teachers will need to help students identify which text frame is most appropriate for the notes, but as

students become experienced with this strategy they will become increasingly able to accomplish this step independently.

ADVANTAGES

Structured Notetaking is a highly effective strategy for a number of reasons:

- Students are able to see relationships between ideas as they take notes—they come to realize that notetaking is more than writing down isolated pieces of information.

- Students are able to take notes that are coherent and easy to use for study and future learning.

- Students are provided with organizational models which teach them the basic structure of the information they are learning.

- Structured notes emphasis visual representation of information, which facilitates memory of the material.

- Student-created structured notes stimulate creativity and make notetaking a more enjoyable activity.

- This strategy can be adapted for students from elementary age through high school and can be successfully used with materials in all content areas.

FURTHER RESOURCES

Cook, D. (Ed.). (1989). *Strategic learning in the content areas.* Madison, WI: Department of Public Instruction.

Smith, P., & Tompkins, G. (October, 1988). Structured notetaking: A new strategy for content area readers. *Journal of Reading,* 46-53.

Test Strategy Outline

Your pulse begins to quicken. Beads of sweat emerge on your forehead. Your hands become cold and clammy. You begin to feel shaky. You can't think straight. Your mind frantically jumps around and you cannot focus on the task at hand. Your performance is falling apart. All that time you put in studying is being wasted. You are blowing another exam!

The above scenario describes the sort of "Stephen King" nightmare that is experienced by many of our students when facing testing situations. "Test Anxiety" is a common complaint among students when they reflect upon their performance on exams. Teachers can help students confront test anxiety through strategies both preparing for exams and taking exams.

Many students do not know how to use their study time for exams effectively. They may not be clear on

---

Awareness of the exam format lets students know whether they will be studying for recognition tasks or recall tasks.

---

what to study and on how to efficiently mobilize their time and resources for the best possible impact. Using a Test Strategy Outline (Buehl, 1994) with students can help them to make decisions about the best way they can prepare for your exams.

THE STRATEGY

Teachers are sometimes amazed at students' failure to pick up classroom cues on what is important and should be studied for exams. And unfortunately, many students wait passively for the teacher to tell them exactly the content of the exam. The following steps will help to develop students who can independently determine what to study and how to study it:

1 Plan a class period before an important exam to have students brainstorm in cooperative groups

specific material they feel will be covered on the exam. As part of this process, have them consult their textbooks, notebooks, study guides, or any other relevant material that might be a source for exam preparation. Ask them to consider what cues help them to determine possible test content (for example, direct statement by the teacher, amount of class time spent on material, emphasis on the material in the textbook, etc.).

Avoid responding to "Will this be on the exam?" questions. Instead, urge the students to use their own understanding of what's important to guide this process. Solicit the ideas from each group and list them on an overhead transparency.

2 Distribute a blank Test Strategy Outline to each student to provide structure for a discussion of study strategy. Start by helping the students target the materials most appropriate as sources for study. Include consideration of sources often neglected by students for exam study: homework, quizzes, lab exercises, small group discussions, and so forth.

3 Next encourage students to ask questions about the nature of the exam. In order to be mentally prepared for the exam format, students should assume responsibility for inquiring as to the mix of question types and how significantly each type will weigh in the scoring of the exam. Awareness of the exam format lets students know whether they will be studying for **recognition** tasks (such as true/false or multiple choice) or **recall** tasks (such as short answer or essay). They should also know to what extent the performance on the exam will effect their grade for the course.

4 Ask the students to suggest possible study strategies for preparing for the exam. As you receive suggestions, list them under one of two headings on an

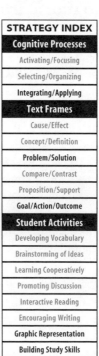

STRATEGY INDEX
Cognitive Processes
Activating/Focusing
Selecting/Organizing
Integrating/Applying
Text Frames
Cause/Effect
Concept/Definition
Problem/Solution
Compare/Contrast
Proposition/Support
Goal/Action/Outcome
Student Activities
Developing Vocabulary
Brainstorming of Ideas
Learning Cooperatively
Promoting Discussion
Interactive Reading
Encouraging Writing
Graphic Representation
Building Study Skills

Test Strategy for:

Current Grade in Course ___ How will this Exam affect your Grade:

Specific Material to be covered on Exam (What will I have to know?):

Study Materials Needed:

___ Textbook
___ Notes
___ Study Guide
___ Work Sheets
___ Homework
___ Quizzes
___ Old Tests
___ Other:

Format of Exam (Check all that apply):
___ Multiple Choice
___ Matching
___ Fill in Blanks

___ True/False
___ Short Answer
___ Essay
___ Problem Solving

___ Definitions
___ Applying Skills
___ Other:

Strategies to be Used for Study (Studying by Looking vs. Studying by Doing)

1.

2.

3.

4.

Study Schedule: Exam will be given on _____.
(List study times and tasks you will be involved in.)

1.

2.

3.

Strategies for Studying for Exams

1. Complete all work that is assigned.

2. Review the readings and notes.

3. Organize material for study:
   • Make 3"x 5" Cards for Vocabulary and Facts
   • Map Important Concepts
   • Organize Notes
   • Create Graphic Organizers (Charts, Diagrams)

4. Think up Possible Exam Questions

5. Make use of Memory Strategies
   • Number Pegs
   • Alphabet Pegs
   • Word Clues
   • Locations (Loci Method)
   • Story Chains
   • Links

6. Study with a Partner

7. Quiz Yourself Frequently

8. Be like a computer—SAVE your work
   in your memory

Studying By Looking

Review Chapter

Review Study Guide

Review Teacher List of What to Know

Review Homework & Assignments

Review Notes

Recite Information (SAVE)

Studying By Doing

Make Index Cards

Create Graphics—Charts, Diagrams, Pictures

Organize Notes into Summaries

Predict & Answer
Exam Questions

Use Memory Strategies

Study With a Partner &
Quiz Each Other

Be the "Expert"—Say It
in Your Own Words

overhead transparency or chalkboard: *"Studying by Looking"* vs. *"Studying by Doing."* Strategies such as reviewing a textbook chapter or reciting from notes would fit under the "Studying by Looking" category.

"Studying by Doing" activities involve some level of reformulating material, such as using index cards for review, creating graphic organizers such as charts or diagrams, developing summary sheets from notes or textbook sections, brainstorming possible exam questions, or making use of memory strategies, such as pegs or links (see pages 117-122 for descriptions of Whole Brain Memory Strategies). Other options include group study or working with a partner.

Emphasize that while both types of study are important, *"Studying by Doing"* activities usually are more active and involve more in-depth processing of the information to be learned. Next discuss a study schedule that allots sufficient time for putting these strategies into action.

5 After the exam, have the students write about their preparation strategies in their notebooks or journals. What ideas worked the best for them, and what parts of the exam gave them the most trouble? How will this experience effect their study for the next exam? Use the Test Strategy Outline with the students for future exams as a prompt for helping them organize their study and approach test taking with more confidence.

ADVANTAGES

Using a Test Strategy Outline with students addresses testing anxiety through thorough preparation. Other advantages include:

- Students become more independent in making connections between what is being learned and how that learning is assessed.

- Students are asked to verbalize how they "read" the teacher and evaluate course materials to determine the priorities of the curriculum.

- Students develop a blueprint for study that will help them enter testing situations more organized and confident.

- Students are encouraged to adopt as part of their study routine strategies that involve more active processing of the material.

FURTHER RESOURCES

Buehl, D. (December, 1994). Test anxiety: Nervous students sometimes blow a test they should ace. *WEAC News & Views*, 13.

Vocabulary Overview Guide

As teachers, we know that vocabulary development is a critical component of reading comprehension. But many of the activities we use with students to improve their vocabularies are not as successful as we would like. Students who are given lists of words to look up and study admit that they forget most of them once the test is over. And learning

---

The Vocabulary Overview Guide is a graphic organizer that includes a meaningful clue as well as definition.

---

new words from reading is a limited way to broaden vocabulary because students tend to "read over" new words and do not stop to take time to examine them.

The Vocabulary Overview Guide (Carr, 1985) is a structured activity that involves students with taking personal responsibility for identifying and learning useful new words from their reading. This strategy conditions students to look for key words as they read and it provides a system for studying the words so that they are retained over time.

THE STRATEGY

The Vocabulary Overview Guide is a graphic organizer that includes a meaningful clue as well as definition (see example). Students are encouraged to develop a strong association between the new word and something that will trigger a sense of its meaning. For instance, a student learning the word *extinct* may select "dinosaurs" as a clue to the meaning "no longer living." A student learning *biceps* may decide upon "Arnold Schwarzenegger" as a meaningful clue. As students study their new words, they start by covering up the definition to see if the clue is sufficient to trigger the word's meaning.

Using the Vocabulary Overview Guide involves the following steps:

1 Select a reading assignment that contains a number of words that would be useful for your

students to learn. After they have read the selection, model the Vocabulary Overview Guide using an overhead transparency or chalkboard. For example, key words in a story on ghosts might include *eerie, tormented, apparition, legend, premonition,* and *supernatural*.

2 Discuss with the students the main topic or theme of the selection. Note how the words you have selected have some connection to this topic or theme.

3 Next identify with your students the important categories within this topic. Under the topic of ghosts, you may decide upon: what are ghosts like? (*appearance*), how do people react to ghosts? (*people*), and why are there ghosts? (*explanation*) as your categories. Write these categories on the overview guide, and arrange the key words on the guide under the appropriate category (see "Ghosts" example).

4 Assign individual students to look up the definitions of each new word. Then with your students, brainstorm possible clues to help them learn each new word. These clues help students link the new word to their background knowledge. For example, students may decide that *eerie* might describe how they would feel being in a cemetery at midnight. This becomes their meaningful clue for remembering this word.

Encourage students to personalize their clues. A clue that works for one student may not connect with another. For example, students unfamiliar with Dickens' *A Christmas Carol* will not find the clue of Mr. Scrooge helpful for remembering the meaning of *apparition*. However, the movie *Ghostbusters* could be just the clue to trigger this word.

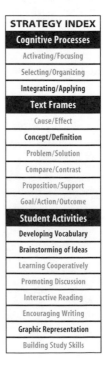

STRATEGY INDEX

Cognitive Processes
- Activating/Focusing
- Selecting/Organizing
- **Integrating/Applying**

Text Frames
- Cause/Effect
- **Concept/Definition**
- Problem/Solution
- Compare/Contrast
- Proposition/Support
- Goal/Action/Outcome

Student Activities
- **Developing Vocabulary**
- **Brainstorming of Ideas**
- Learning Cooperatively
- Promoting Discussion
- Interactive Reading
- Encouraging Writing
- **Graphic Representation**
- Building Study Skills

Vocabulary Overview Guide for a Story on Ghosts

Topic: _Ghosts_

Category:	Appearance	People	Explanation
	eerie	_tormented_	_legend_
	Clue: cemetery at midnight	**Clue:** victim	**Clue:** Paul Bunyan
	DEFINITION: frightening / strange	DEFINITION: to be pained / to be bothered	DEFINITION: a story from the / past; may not be / true
	apparition	_premonition_	_supernatural_
	Clue: Mr. Scrooge	**Clue:** storm clouds	**Clue:** Superman
	DEFINITION: ghostly figure	DEFINITION: a warning / a feeling something / will happen	DEFINITION: something outside / the natural world
	Clue:	**Clue:**	**Clue:**
	DEFINITION:	DEFINITION:	DEFINITION:

5 Gradually move toward requiring more student responsibility for identifying, categorizing, and defining new key words from a reading. You could move from identifying some of the new words with the whole class to assigning these tasks to be done in small groups or with student pairs. Finally, individual students should be able to construct their own Vocabulary Overview Guides based on a reading assignment.

ADVANTAGES

The Vocabulary Overview Guide offers a number of advantages to the classroom teacher:

- Students develop ownership of the new words that they are encountering and learning.

- Students are provided with a well organized structure for keeping track of and studying key words.

- Students come to regard vocabulary learning as being something more than merely looking up definitions in a dictionary, and they look for ways to link the new word with something they already know.

- Students are more motivated to learn words that they have personally selected from a reading.

- The Vocabulary Overview Guide is a strategy adaptable to all content areas, including science, social studies, and math.

FURTHER RESOURCES

Carr, E.G. (1985). The vocabulary overview guide: A metacognitive strategy to improve vocabulary comprehension and retention. *Journal of Reading, 21*(8), 684-689.

Cook, D. (Ed.). (1989). *Strategic learning in the content areas.* Madison, WI: Department of Public Instruction.

Whole Brain Memory Strategies— Link and Loci

"*I read it, but I don't remember!*" "*I studied last night, but I still forgot it when I took the test.*" "*I guess I am one of those people who has a bad memory.*"

Teachers field comments like these almost daily from students frustrated with their attempts to retain what they are learning. Many students come to regard the ability to remember as something you are born with—either you are someone with a "good memory" or you're not.

Recitation tends to be the strategy most frequently used by students confronted with memory tasks. Yet,

---

Whole Brain Memory Strategies involve students in using creativity, vivid associations, and visual imagery.

---

while repeating information does enhance remembering it, merely going over material a number of times is not the most effective way to approach many of the memory demands students face. In contrast, Whole Brain Memory Strategies involve students in using creativity, vivid associations, and visual imagery, which are often referred to as "right brain" activities, in addition to the more traditional emphasis on verbal processing of the material, typically described as "left brain" mental work.

In their still popular best seller, *The Memory Book*, Lorayne and Lucas (1974) discuss a number of memory systems that help students both to store information into their long-term memories and to retrieve that information when it is readily needed. Two such systems are the Link strategy and the Loci method. The Link strategy involves creating vivid associations between information that is connected in some sort of meaningful way. The Loci method dates back to the ancient Greeks, who associated information such as key parts of a memorized oration with specific locations they could visualize in their minds.

THE STRATEGIES

Whole Brain Memory Strategies such as the Link and Loci require personal experimentation and practice in stimulating the imagination. Using these strategies with students involve the following steps:

1 Introduce the memory systems through "warm up" exercises that provide students with opportunities to explore their use of mental imagery. Ask the students to relax, close their eyes, and try to imagine what is suggested to them by using all their senses of sight, touch, taste, sound, and smell. The following imagery exercise is an example:

> *Imagine that you are sitting in front of an extra-large pizza. Look at it very carefully. What container is it in? What shape is it? What kind of toppings do you see? How are they arranged on the pizza? What colors do you see? What kind of crust does it have? How does it smell? Reach down and select a piece to taste. Is it a square piece or a triangle? Is it hot to the touch? What do you notice about the melted cheese as you lift the piece? How does it feel on your tongue and in your mouth when you take a bite? Imagine what that bite of pizza taste like.*

2 Next, model use of memory strategies with concrete information that will be easy for students to "see in their mind's eye." A series of paired words to be remembered provides excellent practice for teaching students the Link strategy. Suggest exaggerated, humorous, even outrageous images to students that will help them "link" the paired words. Encourage stu-

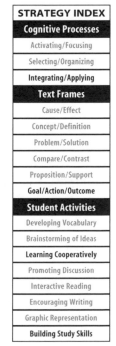

STRATEGY INDEX

Cognitive Processes
Activating/Focusing
Selecting/Organizing
Integrating/Applying

Text Frames
Cause/Effect
Concept/Definition
Problem/Solution
Compare/Contrast
Proposition/Support
Goal/Action/Outcome

Student Activities
Developing Vocabulary
Brainstorming of Ideas
Learning Cooperatively
Promoting Discussion
Interactive Reading
Encouraging Writing
Graphic Representation
Building Study Skills

dents to imagine some sort of out-of-the-ordinary interaction between the two words, filling in as much detail as possible.

For example, with the paired words *elephant/violin*, suggest an elephant playing a familiar tune, loudly and horribly, on the violin, perhaps holding the bow with its trunk. For the paired words *newspaper/pickle*, suggest biting into a giant green pickle which is made from newsprint, each pickle having headlines and stories still imprinted on its outer surface. After providing several word pairs and suggesting bizarre associations, quiz the students by giving them the first word of each pair and have them supply the second. Then reverse the process. The system should work as effectively either way; hearing one word should automatically trigger memory of its pair.

3 The students are now ready to apply the Link strategy to remembering meaningful information they are learning in class. This strategy is an excellent system for use with items that need to be remembered in conjunction with each other. Have students work with partners to develop strong and memorable associations between linked items for the following tasks:

- **Vocabulary Definitions**—students create links between a term and key parts of a definition. For example, to remember that *rampant* means "spreading unchecked over a wide area," students could visualize whole areas covered with elaborate parking ramps through which one drives endlessly. In science, students might link *metacarpals* (bones in the hand) with "your hands **met** the steering wheel when you drove the **car**," and *metatarsals* (bones in the foot) with "your feet **met** the **tar** when you walked."

- **English/Foreign Language Equivalents**—students establish images for hard to remember words and build associations between these images. For example, students learning French may recall that *eau* (pronounced "oh") means water if they imagine loudly saying "oh" as they sink into a tub of hot water or pouring water on their Cheerios for breakfast.

- **Content Knowledge**—students develop mental links between associated information. For example, in social studies, students remember Bell as the inventor of the telephone by imagining a

telephone that rings with church bells. They imagine the movie character Crocodile Dundee eating a can of berries to recall that Canberra is the capital of Australia.

4 At this point, students can also begin to apply the Loci method. Interestingly, the Greek word for location or place is *topos*, the root word of topic. Thus, the Loci method was the source of common turns of speech like "my next topic (place) is…" or "in the first place… ." Key information, especially that which needs to be remembered in a particular order, is associated with various "places" or locations that one can visualize.

Ask the students to relax, close their eyes, and walk in their minds through a familiar location, such as their home. Have them make a mental journey from room to room, "seeing" as much detail in each location as they possibly can, including furnishings and other items that would appear in this location.

Next have them associate a key word or image in each location. For example, to recall the periods

---

Students establish images for hard to remember words and build associations between these images.

---

of classical music, students might imagine a "runny sauce" (Renaissance) glopped all over their first location, several major pieces of furniture "broke" (Baroque) in their second, stacks of "classified documents" (Classical) in their third, someone doing something "romantic" (Romantic) in their fourth, Robin Williams doing his "impressions" (Impressionistic) in the fifth, and so on.

Possible locations for the Loci method are virtually unlimited, from the houses on your block to the positions on a baseball team. Suggest that students experiment with a wide variety of locations when involved in memory work.

ADVANTAGES

Whole Brain Memory Strategies sometimes strike teachers as frivolous gimmicks which don't really involve truly learning the material. Certainly material has to be understood if it is to be useful to students.

But memory strategies such as the Link and Loci can be powerful tools for learning because:

- Students are stimulated to use all their senses, to think visually as well as verbally, and to bring their imaginations to bear on memory tasks.

- Students find Whole Brain Memory Strategies fun to experiment with, and they are motivated to spend time engaged with committing important material into their memories.

- Students are empowered by these strategies, as they discover that they really can learn and remember useful information.

- Students receive explicit training on how to tap into their personal memory potentials and they develop personalized systems for remembering.

- Whole Brain Memory Strategies can be applied with students at all levels, from elementary age through high school.

FURTHER RESOURCES

Lorayne, H., & Lucas, J. (1974). *The memory book.* New York, NY: Stein and Day.

Whole Brain Memory Strategies— Pegs

"**W**ho played for the Milwaukee Brewers on their 1982 World Series team?" How would a Wisconsin baseball fan go about remembering these players? Almost without exception, baseball fans would turn to a memory strategy to help them recollect these names—they would use each position on the baseball diamond as a cue. "Let's see...there was Cecil Cooper at first base, Jim Gantner at second, Robin Yount at short, Paul Molitor at third..." and so on. They would be taking advantage of memory pegs.

Pegs might be seen as a row of mental mailboxes into which material can be placed for storage and retrieval.

Peg systems are examples of Whole Brain Memory Strategies. Two popular Whole Brain Memory Strategies—the Link and Loci Methods—combine imagination and visualization as key components for enhancing memory (see page 117). A third successful method, Peg Memory Systems, uses associations with items that occur in a particular sequence to trigger the recall of information. Pegs might be seen as a row of mental mailboxes into which material can be placed for storage and retrieval. Numbers, letters of the alphabet, months of the year, days of the week— all can be integrated into a peg memory system.

THE STRATEGIES

Whole Brain Memory Strategies are based on the use of mental imagery and creativity. Peg Systems, which date back to the seventeenth century, can be introduced to students in the following way:

1 Start with a simple peg system, such as the numbers from one to ten. A concrete image, something that students can readily visualize, is assigned to each number. Suggest key images that rhyme with the number: one/bun; two/shoe; three/tree; four/door; five/hive; six/sticks; seven/heaven; eight/plate; nine/spine; ten/hen. Review each of these rhymes with the students so that they can quickly remember the key image that corresponds with each number.

2 Next, have the students memorize ten items in order by creating a mental connection between the key image for each number and something that can be visualized for each item. Model creating images for the first few items to the entire class. Then have students work with partners to develop images for the rest of the list.

For example, students learning the eleven states comprising the Confederacy during the American Civil War could use the number peg system. The first peg (bun) is linked to two states: North and South Carolina. Suggest two giant hot dog buns, one in a blue jacket (North) and the other in gray (South), who are loudly singing a popular Christmas carol outside your home. The second peg (shoe) is linked to Mississippi—a refined young Miss is sipping a drink from a shoe. The third peg (tree) and Florida are connected by an image of a floor made of tree trunks.

As the students work with a partner they create images for the rest of the states. Encourage them to develop vivid, bizarre, and outrageous connections, which make the images more memorable. Students might imagine loudly bamming a door shut (four—Alabama); George Bush pursued by stinging bees (five—Georgia); whacking the St. Louis Cardinals baseball team with sticks (six—Louisiana); Angels named Tex wearing ten gallon hats with halos (seven— Texas); and so on for Virginia, Arkansas, and Tennessee.

The Number Peg system is especially useful for remembering ordered information, and students have successfully applied this method to learning in a variety of diverse situations,

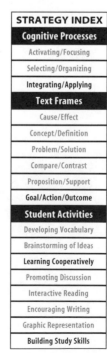

STRATEGY INDEX
Cognitive Processes
Activating/Focusing
Selecting/Organizing
Integrating/Applying
Text Frames
Cause/Effect
Concept/Definition
Problem/Solution
Compare/Contrast
Proposition/Support
Goal/Action/Outcome
Student Activities
Developing Vocabulary
Brainstorming of Ideas
Learning Cooperatively
Promoting Discussion
Interactive Reading
Encouraging Writing
Graphic Representation
Building Study Skills

Alphabet Memory Pegs

a	ape	**n**	envelope
b	bee	**o**	bowl of Cheerios
c	sea	**p**	pea
d	demon	**q**	pool cue
e	eel	**r**	arm
f	fan	**s**	snake saying "sssss"
g	jeans	**t**	tea
h	hat	**u**	unicorn
i	eye	**v**	planet Venus
j	blue jay	**w**	Bucky Badger with W
k	cake	**x**	x-ray
l	elf	**y**	wine
m	McDonalds	**z**	zebra

Number Memory Pegs

1	bun	**6**	sticks
2	shoe	**7**	heaven
3	tree	**8**	plate
4	door	**9**	spine
5	hive	**10**	hen

from identifying each amendment of the Bill of Rights to memorizing the Ten Commandments in Sunday School.

3 The students are now ready to experiment with other possible memory pegs. One system that can be used for larger arrays of information is the Alphabet Peg system. Each letter of the alphabet is assigned a concrete image, which is then linked to information to be remembered. Using an image which contains the sound of the letter is a popular way to develop an Alphabet Peg system. For example, a=ape, b=bee, c=sea, and so on. (See the Alphabet Pegs List for suggestions for all 26 letters and Number Pegs List for numbers one through ten.) Students could also assign an image which begins with the letter (a=apple; b=bear; c=cat, and so on).

The students could use Alphabet Pegs for remembering extensive information, like the Presidents of United States, major events in a story or historical period, countries included a certain geographical area of the world, states and their capitals, characteristics of biological classifications, or other such lists of arbitrary items.

For example, students studying the Civil War could use Alphabet Pegs to order important events of that conflict. The first event, the formation of the Confederacy, is linked to the "a" peg: an ape is wearing a gray uniform and waving a confederate flag. Next is Fort Sumter: bees ("b") are sitting at desks in their hive calculating math sums. The battle of First Bull Run is remembered by imagining the Chicago Bulls basketball team playing a game in the sea ("c"). The system would permit students to retain an entire chronology of the war that is easy to recall.

4 Introduce the students to other possible pegs for memory. For example, the months of the year provide twelve pegs for information. Some students use a major holiday or event as the image for each month: January/New Year's Celebration; February/Valentine's Day; March/St. Patrick's Day; April/Easter; May/Memorial Day; June/Summer Vacation; July/4th of July; August/Back to School; September/Labor Day; October/Halloween; November/Thanksgiving; December/Christmas.

The days of the week provide students with seven pegs. Students learning the system of biological classification can use this peg system: Monday—a king sitting on the moon (kingdom); Tuesday—cutting 2's into wood with a file (phylum); Wednesday—a wedding between all the members of the class (class); Thursday—ordering drink after drink because you are thirsty (order); Friday—a family of French Fries (family); Saturday—a genius sat on a tack (genus); Sunday—the sun is speaking (species).

Encourage your students to identify other possible pegs—members of a group such as family or friends, athletic teams, the lineup of television programs on a specific evening, songs by a favorite singer, and others—that they can personalize for use in memory tasks.

ADVANTAGES

Peg Systems offer similar advantages to other Whole Brain Memory Strategies :

- Students are stimulated to use all their senses, to think visually as well as verbally, and to employ their imaginations when confronted with memory tasks.

- Students enjoy experimenting with Whole Brain Memory Strategies, and they are motivated to use their creativity when committing important material into their memories.

- Modeling use of memory strategies with students helps them discover that they really can learn and remember useful information.

- Students develop strategies for learning information that must be remembered in a particular order.

- Whole Brain Memory Strategies can be applied with students at all levels, from elementary age through high school.

FURTHER RESOURCES

Higbee, K. (1977). *Your memory: How it works and how to improve it*. Englewood Cliffs, NJ: Prentice Hall.

Lorayne, H., & Lucas, J. (1974). *The memory book*. New York, NY: Stein and Day.

References and Strategy Graphic Organizers

References

Alvermann, D. (1991). The discussion web: A graphic aid for learning across the curriculum. *The Reading Teacher, 45*(2), 92-99.

Bagley, M. (1987). *Imagery to develop memory.* Monroe, NY: Trillium Press.

Beck, I., & McKeown, M. (November/December,1981). Developing questions that promote comprehension: The story map. *Language Arts,* 913-918.

Blachowicz, C. (November, 1993). *Developing active comprehenders.* Paper presented at the meeting of the Madison Area Reading Council.

Buehl, D. (Spring, 1992). The connection overview: A strategy for learning in science. *WSRA Journal,* 21-30.

Buehl, D. (1992). A frame of mind for reading history. *The Exchange. Secondary Reading Interest Group Newsletter,*5(1).

Buehl, D., & Hein, D. (1990). Analogy graphic organizer. *The Exchange. Secondary Reading Interest Group Newsletter, 3*(2).

Buehl, D. (May, 1991). Fact pyramids. *New perspectives: Reading across the curriculum.*

Carr, E.G., & Ogle, D. (1987). KWL plus: A strategy for comprehension and summarization. *Journal of Reading, 30*(7), 626-631.

Carr, E.G. (1985). The vocabulary overview guide: A metacognitive strategy to improve vocabulary comprehension and retention. *Journal of Reading, 21*(8), 684-689.

Cook, D. (Ed.). (1986). *A guide to curriculum planning in reading.* Madison, WI: Wisconsin Department of Public Instruction.

Cook, D. (Ed.). (1989). *Strategic learning in the content areas.* Madison, WI: Wisconsin Department of Public Instruction.

Frayer, D., Frederick, W., & Klausmeier, H. (1969) A schema for testing the level of cognitive mastery. *Working Paper No. 16.* Madison, WI: Wisconsin Research and Development Center.

Hayes, D. (November, 1989). Helping students GRASP the knack of writing summaries. *Journal of Reading,* 96-101.

Higbee, K. (1977). *Your memory: How it works and how to improve it.* Englewood Cliffs, N.J.: Prentice Hall.

Johnson, D., & Pearson, P. (1984). *Teaching reading vocabulary, 2nd edition,* Holt, Rinehart, & Winston.

Kennedy, M. (May, 1991). Policy issues in teacher education. *Phi Delta Kappan.*

Kinkead, D., Thompson, R., Wright, C., & Gutierrez, C. (1992). Pyramiding: Reading and writing to learn social studies. *The Exchange. Secondary Reading Interest Group Newsletter, 5*(2).

Klein, M. (1988). *Teaching reading comprehension and vocabulary: A guide for teachers.* Englewood Cliffs, NJ: Prentice Hall.

Langer, J. (1984). Examining background knowledge and text comprehension, *Reading Research Quarterly,* 19.

Lazear, D. (1991).*Seven ways of teaching: The artistry of teaching with multiple intelligences.* Palatine, IL.: Skylight Publishing.

Lorayne, H., & Lucas, J. (1974). *The memory book.* New York: Stein and Day.

McNeil, J. (1984). *Reading comprehension: New directions for classroom practice.* Glenview, IL. Scott, Foresman, and Company.

Moore, D., & Moore, S. (1986). *Possible sentences* in E. Dishner, T. Bean, J. Readence, & D. Moore (Eds.), *Reading in the content areas: Improving classroom instruction* (2nd ed.). Dubuque, IA: Kendall/Hunt.

Moore, D., Readence, J., & Rickelman, R. (1989). *Prereading activities for content area reading and learning*, (2nd ed.) Newark, DE: International Reading Association.

Pittelman, S., Heimlich, J., Berglund, R., & French, M. (1991). *Semantic feature analysis: Classroom applications*, Newark, DE: International Reading Association.

Readence, J., Bean, T., & Baldwin, R. (1989). *Content area reading: An integrated approach* (3rd ed.). Dubuque, IA: Kendall/Hunt Publishing Company.

Santa, C. (1988). *Content reading including study systems*. Dubuque, IA: Kendall/Hunt Publishing.

Schwartz, R., & Raphael, T. (1985). Concept of definition: A key to improving students' vocabulary. *The Reading Teacher, 39*, 676-682.

Smith, P., & Tompkins, G. (October,1988). Structured notetaking: A new strategy for content area readers. *Journal of Reading*, 46-53.

Solon, C. (1980). The pyramid diagram: A college study skills tool. *Journal of Reading, 23*(7).

Vacca, R. & Vacca, J. (1993). *Content area reading* (4th ed.).New York: Harper Collins College Publishers.

Vaughan, J. & Estes, T. (1986). *Reading and reasoning beyond the primary grades.* Boston: Allyn and Bacon.

Wood, K. (1988). Guiding students through informational text. *The Reading Teacher, 41*(9), 912-920.

Wood, K., Lapp, D., & Flood, J. (1992). *Guiding readers through text: A review of study guides*, Newark, DE: International Reading Association.

WEAC "Reading Room" Columns

Buehl, D. (December, 1994) Test anxiety: Nervous students sometimes blow a test they should ace. *WEAC News and Views.*

————. (November, 1994) Memory aids: Here's a creative strategy pegged to success.*WEAC News and Views.*

————. (September, 1994) Unforgettable: Tricks help students remember material. *WEAC News and Views.*

————. (June, 1994) You said it: Colorful quotes can be the voice of a character's soul. *WEAC News and Views.*

————. (May, 1994) Persona: Character analysis sheds light on story's meaning. *WEAC News and Views.*

————. (April, 1994) Cruising: 'Maps' help students navigate through story elements. *WEAC News and Views.*

————. (February, 1994) Tap into students' natural curiosity. *WEAC News and Views.*

————. (December, 1993) Magnetized: Students are drawn to technique that identifies key words. *WEAC News and Views.*

————. (September, 1993) A note-taking strategy worth noting. *WEAC News and Views.*

————. (June, 1993) Anticipation can lead to edification. *WEAC News and Views.*

————. (May, 1993) Guided imagery triggers visualization, *WEAC News and Views.*

————. (April, 1993) Maps help kids find best definition. *WEAC News and Views.*

————. (March, 1993) In a word: Strategy turns key words into complete thoughts. *WEAC News and Views*, March.

————. (February, 1993) If you could only see things my way. *WEAC News and Views.*

References

————. (December, 1992) Analogies: The intellectual highways that connect concepts with realities. *WEAC News and Views*.

————. (November, 1992) Pyramid helps reader get the point. *WEAC News and Views*.

————. (September, 1992) Outline helps students analyze credibility of author's premise. *WEAC News and Views*.

————. (June, 1992) LINK is not missing in this strategy. *WEAC News and Views*.

————. (May, 1992) A SMART approach to reading. *WEAC News and Views*.

————. (April, 1992) Save the last word for me. *WEAC News and Views*.

————. (March, 1992) 'Big picture' is worth 1,000 words with the connection overview. *WEAC News and Views*.

————. (February, 1992) All students get caught in discussion web. *WEAC News and Views*.

————. (December, 1991) Change frame strategy helps kids find meaning in what they read. *WEAC News and Views*.

————. (November, 1991) Frayer model puts concepts to paper. *WEAC News and Views*.

————. (September, 1991) System helps link words & concepts. *WEAC News and Views*.

————. (June, 1991) A '90's strategy: Be an active reader. *WEAC News and Views*.

————. (May, 1991) Guide is propitious to good vocabulary. *WEAC News and Views*.

———— (April, 1991) RAFT infuses imagination into writing. *WEAC News and Views*.

————. (March, 1991) Add perspective to your reading. *WEAC News and Views*.

————. (February, 1991) Prepping: Being ready from the word 'go.' *WEAC News and Views*.

Analogy Graphic Organizer

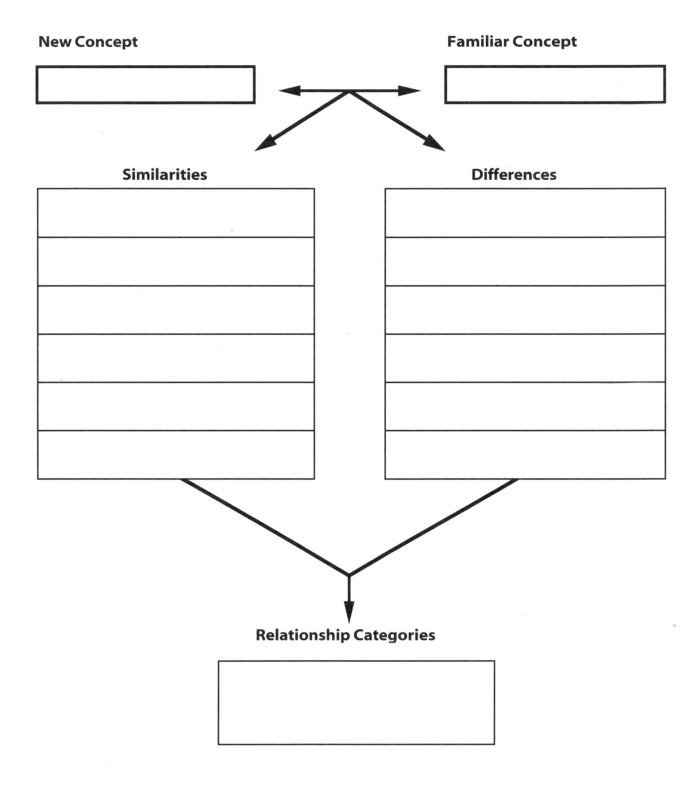

New Concept

Familiar Concept

Similarities

Differences

Relationship Categories

Character Analysis Grid

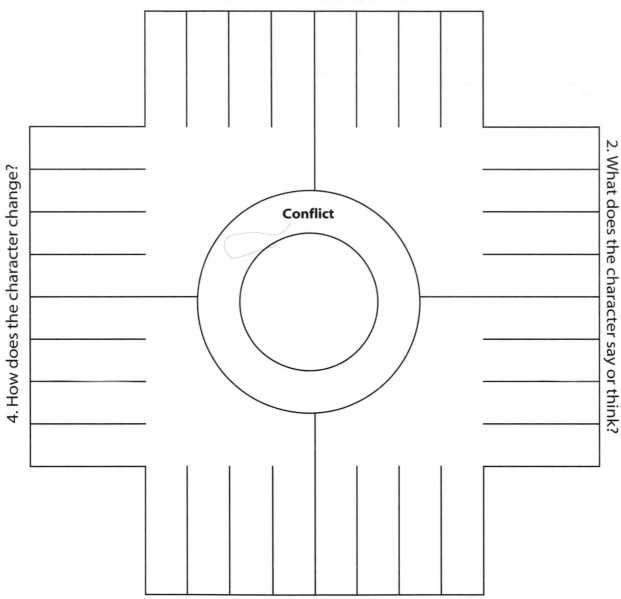

1. What does the character do?

4. How does the character change?

Conflict

2. What does the character say or think?

3. How do others feel about the character?

5. Author's Theme or Point of View:

Concept Definition Map

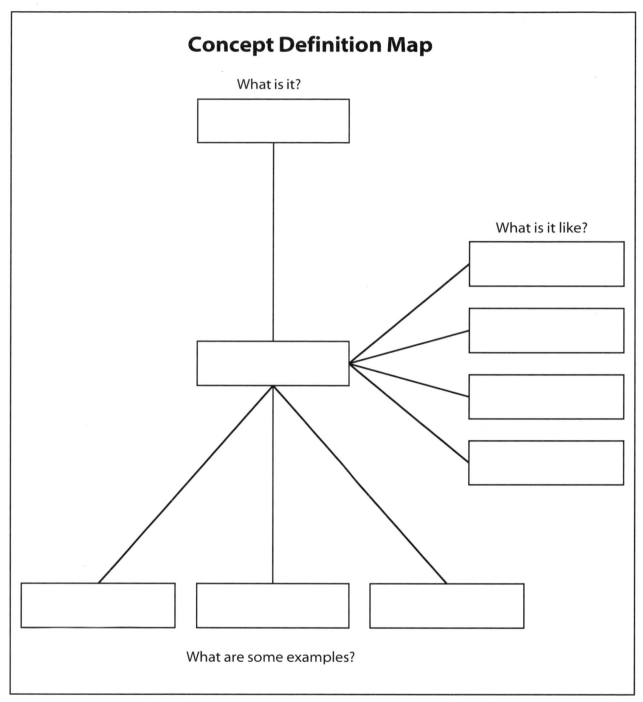

What is it?

What is it like?

What are some examples?

— Schwartz & Raphael (1985)

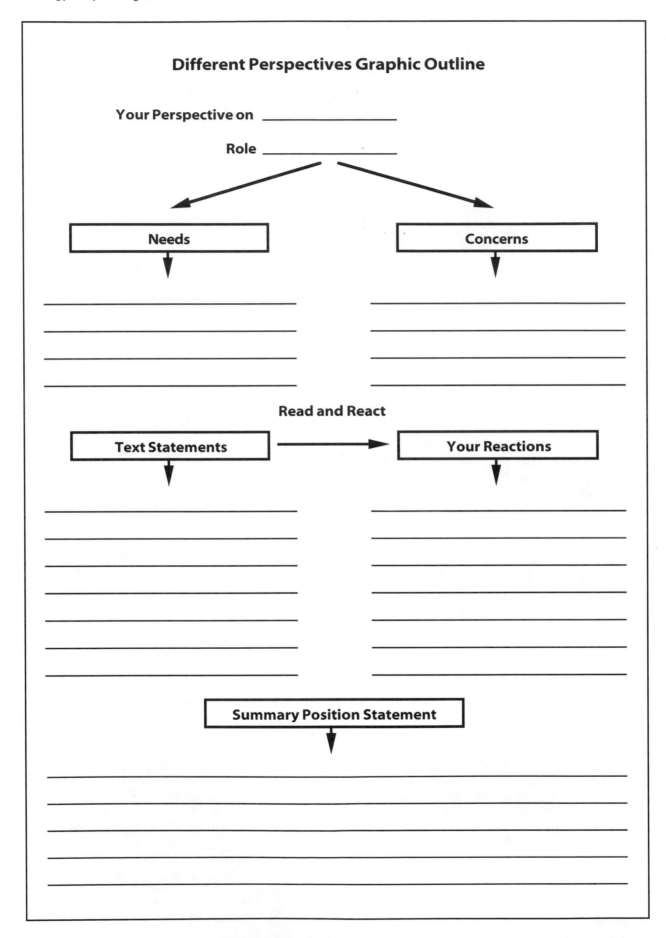

Different Perspectives Graphic Outline

Your Perspective on _____

Role _____

| **Needs** | | **Concerns** |

_____
_____
_____
_____

Read and React

| **Text Statements** | → | **Your Reactions** |

Summary Position Statement

Discussion Web

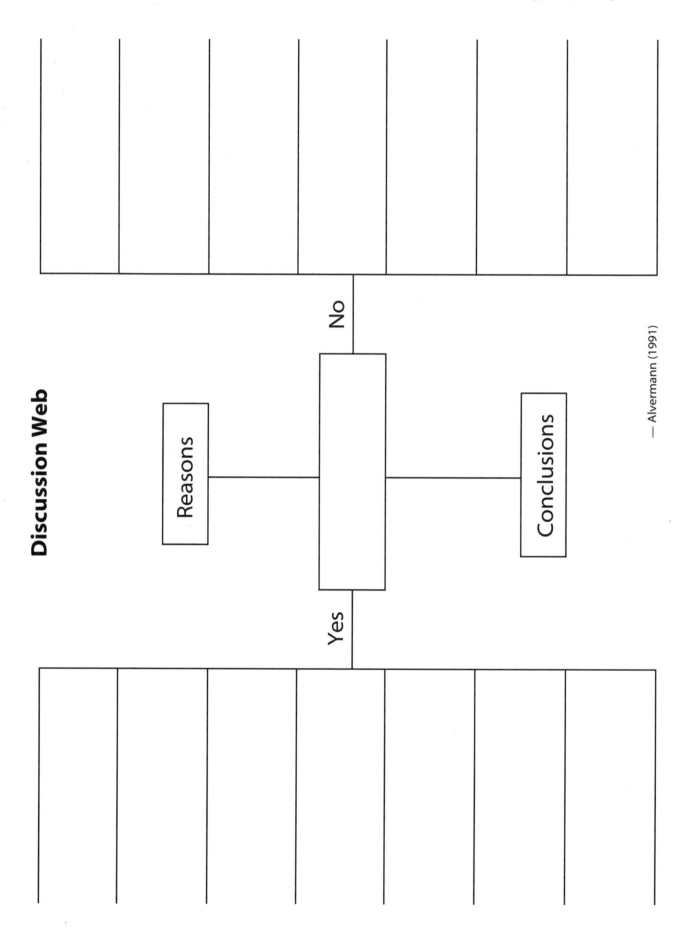

Reasons

Conclusions

No

Yes

— Alvermann (1991)

Frayer Model

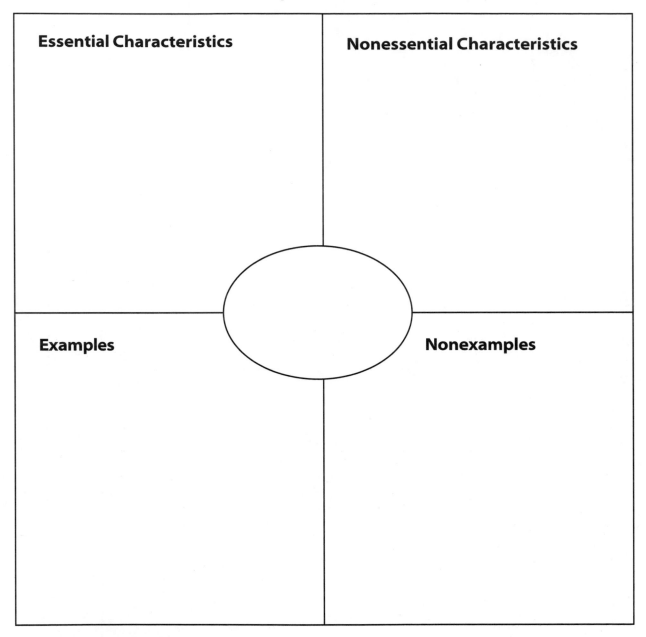

Essential Characteristics

Nonessential Characteristics

Examples

Nonexamples

Change Frame Graphic Organizer

Who?	Who?	Who?
What problems did they face?	What problems did they face?	What problems did they face?
What changes caused these problems?	What changes caused these problems?	What changes caused these problems?
What did they do to solve the problems?	What did they do to solve the problems?	What did they do to solve the problems?

Proposition/Support Outline

Proposition:

Support:

1. Facts
2. Statistics
3. Examples
4. Expert Authority
5. Logic and Reasoning

Connection Overview Graphic Organizer

What's Familiar?

What's the Connection? Skim & Survey the Chapter for things that are familiar and connect with your life or world. List them below:

What topics are covered?

Read the Summary. What topic areas seem to be the most important?

What questions do you have?

Questions of Interest. What questions do you have about this material that may be answered in the chapter?

How is it organized?

Chapter Organization: What categories of information are provided in this chapter?

Translate

Read and Translate: Use 3x5 Cards for Vocabulary.

Semantic Feature Analysis Grid

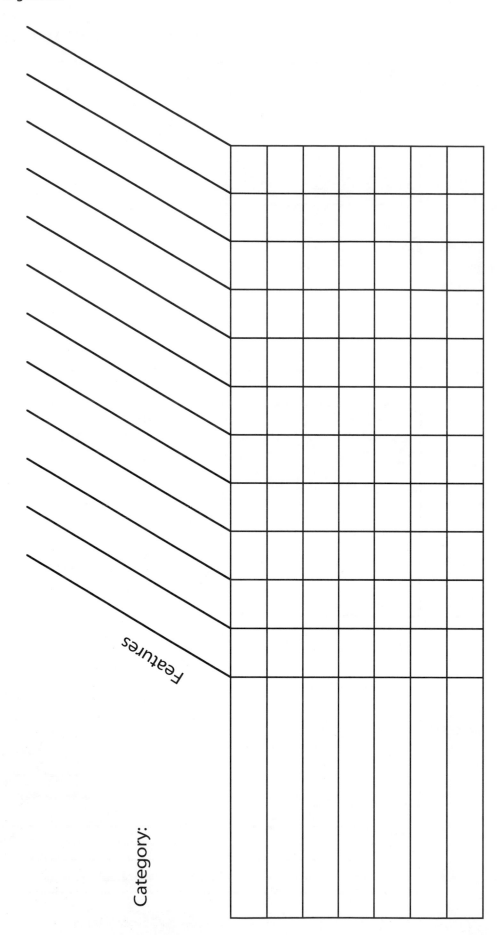

Features

Category:

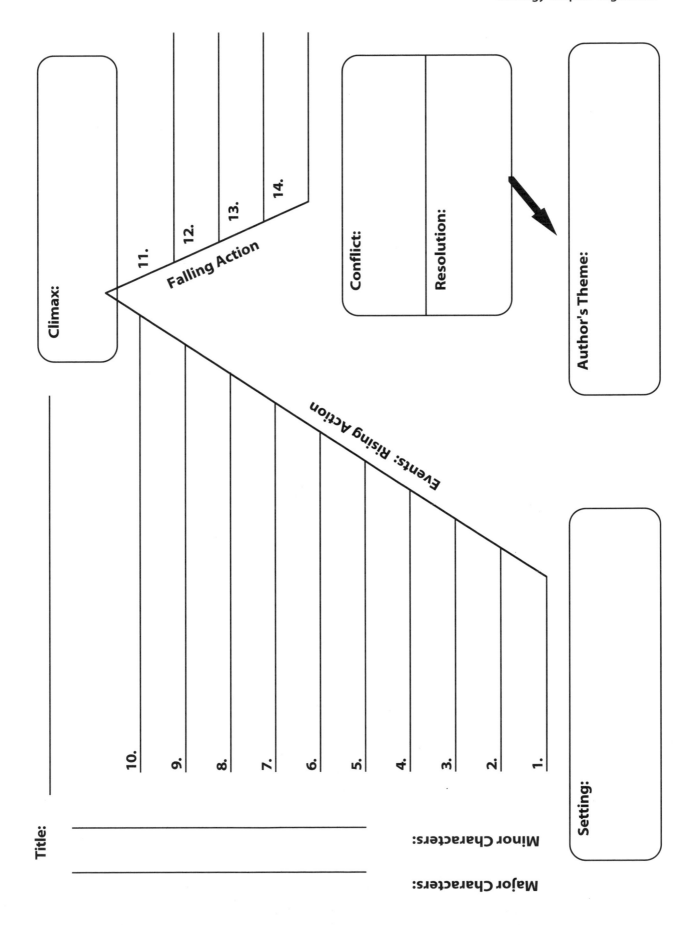

Author's Theme:

Conflict:

Resolution:

Climax:

Falling Action

11.

12.

13.

14.

Events: Rising Action

10.

9.

8.

7.

6.

5.

4.

3.

2.

1.

Title:

Minor Characters:

Major Characters:

Setting:

Test Strategy for:

Current Grade in Course ___ How will this Exam affect your Grade:

Specific Material to be covered on Exam (What will I have to know?):

Study Materials Needed:

___ Textbook
___ Notes
___ Study Guide
___ Work Sheets
___ Homework
___ Quizzes
___ Old Tests
___ Other:

Format of Exam (Check all that apply):
___ Multiple Choice
___ Matching
___ Fill in Blanks

___ True/False
___ Short Answer
___ Essay
___ Problem Solving

___ Definitions
___ Applying Skills
___ Other:

Strategies to be Used for Study (<u>Studying by Looking</u> vs. <u>Studying by Doing</u>)

1.

2.

3.

4.

Study Schedule: Exam will be given on _____.
(List study times and tasks you will be involved in.)

1.

2.

3.

Vocabulary Overview Guide

Topic: _____

Category: _____   _____   _____

Clue: [   ]   Clue: [   ]   Clue: [   ]
      DEFINITION: DEFINITION: DEFINITION:

Clue: [   ]   Clue: [   ]   Clue: [   ]
      DEFINITION: DEFINITION: DEFINITION:

Clue: [   ]   Clue: [   ]   Clue: [   ]
      DEFINITION: DEFINITION: DEFINITION:

— Carr (1985)

··· *Notes* ···